*Tracks in the ... ...ing the
Last Great Fur Boom*

Tracks in the Mud:
Trailing the Last Great Fur Boom

Gene Stark

NORTH STAR PRESS OF ST. CLOUD, INC.
St. Cloud, Minnesota

ISBN: 978-0-87839-630-6

Copyright © 2012 Gene Stark

All rights reserved.

First Edition, September 2012

Printed in the United States of America

Published by
North Star Press of St. Cloud, Inc.
P.O. Box 451
St. Cloud, Minnesota 56302

www.northstarpress.com

TABLE OF CONTENTS

Cold Dreams and Hanging Sparrows 1
Shaky Wheels, Heaven Scent 7
Breakthroughs and Fender 'Rats 14
Flat-tail Days 21
A B.A. and a P.H.D. While Packing Heat in the Dorm 30
Wading into a Cornhusker Classroom 35
Engaging a Wife and Adopting a State 45
The Fur Boom: A Work in Progress 55
A Blue Moon Rising 66
Part-time Bliss, Riding the Learning Curve 75
A New Baby and Old Dreams 84
New Days, Old Ways, in the Golden Haze 92
Heavy Lifting 101
Pure Nirvana, Good Bucks, and a Break 107
The Frosting on the Cake and Kill-dogs on the Prairie 114
Summer Wisdom, Eternal Gifts 119
A Lucky Split and New Horizons 127
Wheeling and Dealing, Grading and Trading 138
Wild Trails 147
New Red Fords and Barred Windows 154
Tracks North 166
Post Boom Days 172

1960s winter red fox-snowshoes required.

Chapter 1

"Cold Dreams and Hanging Sparrows"

I FIND IT FUNNY HOW the memories of a six-year-old go back to a rusty old number one Victor long-spring trap. It was one that was too old to warrant use on my older brother's trap line. Its spring was thin and weak from years of rusting in the water of nearby marshes and lakes. The dog which fits into the notch on the pan had long rusted away. I put a piece of twisted wire in its place so the trap would actually function. The best thing was I could actually set it by pressing the spring with my foot and place the wire over the jaw and into the notch. My equipment was pretty simple. Besides the old number one long-spring, I had a pair of brown, cotton "Jersey" gloves, and I wore a pair of four-buckle overshoes, well decorated with torn red patches where barbed wire fences got the best of them.

My first trap line consisted of the relic number one long-spring placed upon a flattened stone in a nearby lake which had muskrat droppings on it. I checked this set religiously day after day. Finally, one day the trap was triggered and empty. I was excited to see the quarry finally visited my location. Surely a muskrat would have been caught in my trap if that was what had visited the rock. Soon I became convinced that it must have been a wily mink which stealthily sprung my trap. The very thought of such a prize being in such close proximity to my trap made my heart race. In the 1950s a muskrat was worth about fifty cents. This was a fine chunk of money to a six-year-old boy, but the very thought of a mink with a possible thirty-dollar price for the hide was enough to set a young boy's head spinning. Such money would catapult me from one rusty old trap to a whole string of bright, shiny, new Victors and a future of fortune.

Certainly money was an incentive for a young boy growing up in the country to take up trapping. Odd jobs and paper routes were not easy to come by for earning spending money. Trapping was a way to put a few extra dollars into one's pocket. Yet, even then it really wasn't the money that fueled the obsession with fur. It went much farther than money. Part of it was the books about the mountain men and their freedom loving spirit while trapping beaver along quiet mountain streams.

Another enormous factor in the attraction to trapping was the love I had for the wildlife being the target. I became absolutely enamored with furbearers and their lives in the wild. Getting up close and personal with these animals was so exciting. The very thought of looking at a mink track and trying to figure what the animal was doing, where it was going, and even what it was thinking as it made the trail blew my mind. How to selectively place a trap to catch the animal intended was a mystery that constantly tugged at my intuition. My brother and I grew up with hunting and fishing and all the mysteries and tricks associated with those pursuits. Trapping held a special place in my heart, for it required me to meet the furbearers on their own terms and actually become them, to know them.

Of course fur itself is a beautiful thing. It is soft and warm and luxurious. It gave a kid in rural Minnesota a connection to the world. The furs I harvested would possibly end up being worn by people in New York or London or any number of faraway places that I couldn't even dream of visiting. Yes, trapping could give me a jingle and a tingle. It put a little change into my pocket and gave me excitement beyond reality.

My dad's stories of trapping and his instructions on the art were also a great influence upon me. He knew about trapping muskrats and ran many extensive trap lines over the years. Of course my brother and I inherited his traps when he no longer used them. My dad could still go out and make sets that produced a better catch than we were able to make so we were determined to learn all of his secrets. Many of the traps we got from him were decades old in the 1950s and are still in our possession now in the next century, still working just like new. Of course we were notorious, as are all kids, when it came to losing traps. Some of the old obsolete traps we were able to hang onto are still good ideas and are still working great on the trap line. However, there have also been so many innovations of traps and other related equipment that have improved and streamlined the taking of fur.

Much of the inspiration about trapping that I drew from my dad took the form of his stories of trapping in what he then referred to as the "good old days." He talked of muskrats selling for four dollars or more. That was such an unheard of sum of money for a common furbearer that it seemed like a dream. The days of forty dollars per mink and even five dollars a skunk put me in awe. Such money was unheard of in the fifties and early sixties. Of course one of the most depressing things that he said was that he believed that the fur market was dead and that we would never see such high prices again.

Tracks in the Mud

These were words that dashed my dreams, for I fancied that maybe there would come a day when I could actually make a living as a trapper. I was told to get such silly notions out of my head. My dad was a realist, and he was giving the best advice he could. I still recall doing a paper in elementary school where we were supposed to write about what we would want to do for a living when we grew up. My paper included being a trapper among a couple of other options.

When I was still quite young, I remember the lakes and marshes freezing over and a layer of snow falling to the ground. As the open water trapping came to an end, I still had the great urge to continue trapping. I became a bit obsessed by the weasel. I was fascinated by its change from brown to white as the snow came. I remember my dad saying how the white weasel or ermine was valued in the fur trade. I knew the season ran year round. My great desire was to catch them, so I set out into the willow swamps near our home to trap the wily weasel.

The only trapping method I'd heard of for weasels was to hang a dead bird from a low branch and set the trap under the hanging bird. The weasel would jump after the suspended bird and fall into the trap below. Before I could do this, I had to take my BB gun to the local feed mill and shoot some of the sparrows that fed on the spilt grain.

With my supply of sparrows, string, and number one traps, I headed for the willow swamps. The small double tracks of the weasels were to be found in the willows, as they hunted mice and other rodents. My hanging sparrow sets were made where the tracks seemed fresh. I soon learned that a very important aspect of winter trapping was to keep the traps functional during cold weather, with snow on the ground. I learned that snow is not a good trap covering, as it hardened over the trap, keeping it from springing when a weasel stepped on it. Weasels, being very light on their feet, required a trap which sprang very easily. I had been told that weasels were very wary animals and this kept me from using other coverings, lest I spook the sneaky little critters. It took me a long time to experiment with other trap coverings such as cattail fluff. Finally I had a bit of success and both long-tailed and short-tailed weasels were caught. Some good lessons were learned that later helped me with winter fox trapping. I remember the luster of those fully prime white weasels and how the black tip of their tails contrasted so beautifully with the white fur.

The advertisements in the *Fur-Fish-Game* magazine always intrigued me, especially the ones from fur buyers like Maas and Steffan, in Missouri. We always sold our furs locally, but the advertisements seemed to promise higher prices, and I felt I should send some fur to these folks. A small shipment soon gave me a reality check. I realized they probably advertised their highest prices—the ones they paid for the best quality. My check from them averaged much lower than the prices in the advertisement. One thing I noticed in their price list was that they bought red squirrel skins. Now here was a commodity in good supply in the nearby woods and was virtually unharvested since they really weren't an eating-size squirrel like the fox and gray squirrels we shot.

No local fur buyers bought red squirrels, which are also known as pine squirrels. I figured any price obtained by shipping out of state was better than no price at all. Again the beauty of the red squirrel trapping idea was that they ran all winter and could be trapped after the regular trapping season closed. I spent many cold winter days on skis pursuing the red squirrel. I learned to trap them in the trees where they ran and fed upon acorns and other seeds.

The red squirrel was too small for its skin to fit on a muskrat stretcher, so I fashioned stretchers out of old wire coat hangers and the finished product turned out pretty well. They were stretched fur-in like a mink or muskrat. I remember packing them into a box and shipping them off to Maas and Steffan. All the skeptics in the household said I'd never see a dime from that shipment. A week or two later a check came back. I think that check helped vindicate me from the good-natured jabs from the family about my squirrel skins hanging all over the garage.

Chapter 2

"Shaky Wheels, Heaven Scent"

As I reached the age of about ten, I began to trap with my older brother. Eight years older than I, that of course put wheels into the operation for me instead of having my mother drive me to the lake to set traps. Throughout the rest of elementary school, high school, and college, my brother and I ran trap lines together. He was the very organized, focused type and I was the creative, always-optimistic one. I guess we complemented each other. I remember when muskrat prices went up to around a dollar each, and we really felt that was good money.

One of our more memorable seasons was focused around our only fairly reliable mode of transportation. It was a 1940s vintage pickup truck. I remember the opening day of the trapping season distinctly. We loaded up all of our equipment into the old truck the evening before. I don't remember for sure, but the truck had either a bad starter or a weak battery. We parked the truck on a hill in the driveway so that at five o' clock the next morning we could coast down the incline until we could pop the clutch and get the old girl started. It worked like a charm and she got us to the first lake on our trap line. The season opened at 6:00 a.m., and we had to find a hill to park on near the lake so we could get the truck started again. We managed to set and check a lot of traps with my brother's set of wheels under us. Fortunately there seemed to be a lot of strategically placed hills in our county.

Another memorable day during that season was my first double on mink. It happened while my brother was gone for a few days of deer hunting. Our mom had agreed to transport me to the trap line so I could check the traps in my partner's absence. There were traps to check both before and after school. I remember it like it was yesterday. It was a Wednesday morning on the thirteenth of November. While checking the traps along the north shore on one of our lakes I caught a large buck mink in a pocket set under a tree root and picked up another female a bit farther down the shore. I'll never forget my brother's return that evening when I told him to go down to the basement where we did our skinning and check out the day's catch. He was pleasantly surprised. I remember selling those mink for thirty-two dollars for the male and sixteen dollars for the female. It's amazing how I sometimes have a hard time remembering my wife's birthday, but the price of fur still remains in my mind after all these years.

There are vivid memories of early mornings on the trap line. I can still see the old mink trapper as he pulled up on the gravel road, opened the door on his red International pickup, threw a smoldering straight Camel on the gravel, and crushed it with his left foot. The hip boots he wore were of thick black rubber. He worked the water with bare hands and when he was done there was no sign of a set trap. Of course I couldn't stare, but my glance quickly caught the pile of mink and muskrats in the open bed of his truck.

If I could only ask him just a couple of questions, maybe follow him down a bit of lakeshore or fifty feet of stream; I knew the book of trapping knowledge would instantly open to me and the secrets would pour over me like warm rain. Yet I knew that his tight-lipped manner and business-like actions meant he would never divulge a single trick, and certainly not to a young kid. I knew his secrets would follow him to the grave. Yet I was surprised when he commented upon one of my sets, "Why don't you set your traps under a bit more water, you might catch more mink." I took that comment to heart and it certainly was good advice. The old minker worked in and around my area for years, but I never attained another piece of advice from him. Rumor has it he got arthritis pretty bad, but it did not stop him from trapping. It seems that the long-line mink trapper was always a reality in Minnesota and probably also in many other places as well. We have exceptionally high quality mink in our area and prices for this article never seemed to be too bad. While thirty-dollar mink may not seem like a lot, it was a great sum of money in the fifties and sixties. The old minkers were for the most part a shrewd and secretive bunch. They trapped in some of the same areas we did but we never saw much of what they did on the trap line. Their sets were well hidden, and the rumors of some of their catches were pretty phenomenal. There were some who made a living at it. I remember seeing sixteen mink in one guy's truck and that was pretty early in the morning. They were all freshly caught and I assumed from that morning. At the time I never really thought of the daily wages they made, but thinking back to those days when a dollar an hour was a pretty common wage, they were doing all right. Although raccoon were not as plentiful as they are today, keeping them out of your mink sets was still a good practice. The dollar or two that they brought was hardly worth the hassle and the skinning.

Tracks in the Mud

The hunters still seemed to take the majority of coon then, and of course the sport of coon hunting was very popular at the time. My brother had a friend who owned coon hounds and spent many long and exciting nights following the hounds around in the swamps and woods. Running through dark, prickly ash infested woods was a tough and tumble business. Water trapping was the major part of trapping, with mink and muskrat as the main targets. There was a limited spring beaver season, but beaver were a very rare commodity in southern Minnesota at that time.

Long-haired fur was really out of style in the fifties and early sixties. Raccoon, as formerly stated was relatively cheap and fox were rarely skinned after collecting the bounty that was paid at the time. I remember buyers offering a dollar for prime red fox if they were stretched and dried. When the price went up to around five dollars in the mid-sixties our interest began to rise since there was a pretty solid fox population at the time. Fox weren't something that would draw us from the water in the fall season, but as the lakes and streams froze and the snow came, we began to look with interest at the straight lines of dog-like tracks that followed the shores of our 'rat marshes. Coyotes were almost non-existent at the time, and I suppose that contributed to the large fox population.

Coyotes at that time were found mainly in the central and northern portions of the state. They were mostly called brush wolves to differentiate them from the timber wolves that were and still are found in the northern parts of the state. The "brushies" competed with the timber wolves for range. Then there was still a bounty on the timber wolves in northern Minnesota, and they were hunted and trapped pretty extensively. The guys who trapped the timber wolves were the true "wolfers," a term later adopted by some of the longline coyote takers in the seventies. Soon the timber wolf would be declared "endangered" and instead of being paid a bounty on them, those who killed them could be liable for more jail time than some murderers got. Now, of course there's a movement to move them to "threatened" status so some control can be applied. Maybe modern-day trappers will again be able to harvest limited numbers of the big canines.

We didn't grow up with a lot of fox trapping traditions. Southern Minnesota has always been big water-trapping country and fox were merely something you shot whenever possible or possibly dug out of dens in the spring to collect the bounty.

Pheasant hunters, deer hunters, and bounty hunters accounted for most of the fox harvest that I remember from those times. As our interest grew in catching fox, because of their increasing fur value, we began to research types of sets that would catch them.

A few people did catch some fox in traps around the area and they had a few classic sets that caught the canines. One of the most popular was the old pile set. It consisted of a pile of straw or manure or whatever was handy with traps set on the mound. Bait was placed either near the pile or in some cases people had success in placing the bait in the pile. Fox, of course tend to go to high places to survey the surrounding area and when they went to the top of the mound they were caught. Usually a drag anchored the set and it worked well in the cold snowy weather. Traps could be bedded in dry chaff or cut-up straw and would spring properly. The set worked and was responsible for my first red fox. The sets were not a real streamlined deal and took lots of time and materials to construct. They could be checked from a distance though, and when the pile was tore up you knew you had made a catch.

Following fox tracks probably led us to most of the other sets we tried. Dead furrows along fields, where fox liked to travel accounted for some catches. It was a type of trail set that worked. Fence crossings and sets by natural holes also worked. We discovered that the tops of muskrat houses right after freeze up were great locations and were really a variation on the old mound set. We figured out how to freeze the trap chains into the ice to anchor them so we didn't have to hunt the foxes in the huge cattail sloughs, when the traps were attached to drags. It seems that in our early days of fox trapping we were always dealing with frozen ground or snow situations and we began to learn about keeping traps working in those conditions. Those were helpful lessons and we even began to learn to carry trap bedding materials to keep the sets working.

    I suppose the greatest breakthrough for us in fox trapping was the discovery of dirt trapping techniques. Many books were appearing on the subject, and I suppose the great "secrets" were coming out of the bag. We learned how to make the dirt-hole set, which is still one of the greatest canine producers available. It imitates where another canine has buried something for later and of course any other passing predator will dig it up. We now had a tool in our arsenal that was easy to employ and could be made quickly. The next big learning curve was to determine location without the crutch of snow on the ground. In other words, figure out where the fox ran on their daily travels. We soon realized how extremely important location is when trapping the land-roving canines.

    Fox trapping also began to become an earlier endeavor than previously because dirt sets could be kept working much easier before freezing weather set in. There was no closed season on fox in those years, and we found that the fur was of pretty good quality at the end of October and we could get a dynamite week of good fox trapping done before the water season opened. The smell of skunk still brings memories of the fox lines we ran. Many of the lures we used were based with skunk essence and of course those skunked-up sets always seemed to produce fox.

I'll never forget a close encounter of the skunky kind that occurred before church one Thanksgiving morning. Thanksgiving vacation always was reserved for trapping and as usual I had traps to check before going to church and the traditional visit to close friends of my parents for dinner. I was in a hurry to get traps checked, and in a slight miscalculation during the dispatch of a skunk caught in a set, I received a direct hit of the golden essence. My mom was the most wonderful and understanding person, as she tolerated our outdoor activities, but this was a moment that stretched her patience. I don't think I made it to church, but I did get to the Thanksgiving dinner.

Chapter 3

"Breakthroughs and Fender 'Rats"

OVER THE YEARS SOME REAL breakthroughs have changed the way we trap. The dirt hole for fox was one of those. The Conibear trap was another. I remember trying to set underwater entrances to muskrat dens with regular foothold traps and being frustrated most of the time. We tried pushing them way up into the hole, and I imagine the 'rats swam over them most of the time. We tried blocking them with obstructions to force the swimming animal into the trap, but it worked only rarely. When we first saw the Conibear in the 110 size, we knew immediately it would be deadly on muskrats in underwater den applications. We have many hard-bottomed lakes and the Conibears were dynamite in those dens. We soon totally abandoned conventional feed bed sets on those lakes and just took all the 'rats in the den entrances.

Another innovation that came about was the use of lures and baits. My dad was basically a blind setter, utilizing natural locations that were made no better by use of bait or lure. Feed beds, natural runs, and trails were his only stock in trade. These were fast and efficient sets that proved very effective. He felt that so-called "lures" were bogus gimmicks, and he never put much stock in any kind of bait. Of course being the inquisitive innovator, I read the ads in *Fur-Fish-Game* magazine by lure makers such as E.J. Dailey and S. Hawbacker and Sons and decided to try some lures. As we began to use dirt-hole sets for fox and mound and bait sets for beaver we really saw the effectiveness of lures and baits. This opened a whole new facet of trapping for us, and we began to use the baited pocket or hole set for water trapping, which added many mink and 'coon to the catch. When these baited sets were used in conjunction with good blind sets, we took the majority of fur on our lines. These were the formative years of my education as a trapper. My mind was like a computer hard-drive, with lots of memory and very little stored to that point. Little did I know how important my growing files of data would one day be to my success.

I recall the sobering events of the November of 1963. The assassination of President Kennedy found us with a day off of school. For me it felt like a day meant to be spent outdoors.

We needed a lot of stakes for our marsh trapping to take place over Thanksgiving, and I took a good part of the day to cut long, slender willow stakes for the trap line. I cut them long, because at that time of year you didn't know if you would be trapping on open water from a boat or on frozen marsh ice when Thanksgiving vacation arrived. Under clear blue skies, with near freezing temperatures, I labored with my hatchet and saw among the twelve-foot-tall stand of willows near a lake. I pondered the events of the week, and as awful as the current events seemed, there was a real and stabilizing feeling about working among the trees. It seemed that nothing could take away the land under my boots, and a calm settled upon me that seemed to emanate optimism. So, the trap line has always seemed to be one of the great modifiers in my life. When all the elements of living and history are added up, they can be sifted through the common denominator of the outdoors and add up to the sanity that we all need. The season went on for us. The marshes froze in their usual hesitant manner. Ice would come, and we would anticipate walking on it to set our traps and then a bit of a warm-up would plunge us back into hip-boot mode. Finally, the ice became solid as it always does in Minnesota, and late November saw us chiseling and sliding along the shores.

Mink, muskrats, and raccoon—a day's catch from the water line.

During the sixties the mink and muskrat season usually ran from early November until the end of December. We pursued the water targets until the end of the season, which ended with us trapping muskrats in their houses—mounds of vegetative matter—that dotted the cattail sloughs, which we could do in the years when it was legal to trap muskrats in their houses. If the Conibear trap and the dirt-hole set were breakthroughs for us in methods, I would say the greatest equipment innovation was probably the shoulder-length rubber gloves. The long gauntlets enabled us to place traps in deep water comfortably and accurately, generally making life easier and more bearable on the water trap line. Until then the only rubber gloves we had were the wrist length rubber-coated gloves that we usually filled with ice water while making or tending the first set. Trapping the late season muskrat houses could only be accomplished when the weather turned cold enough to freeze walking-ice on the marshes and that meant making sets in zero temperatures. It was a mean business especially with the old wrist-length gloves that were stiff as boards and usually partly frozen to one's hands. The shoulder-length gloves helped to alleviate some of the extreme pain of house trapping. We could now reach down deep into the houses, clean out the runs, and bring up the wet material to re-seal the houses and keep them from freezing. Hip boots were still the usual foot wear at this time of the season since breaking through the ice around muskrat houses was not unheard of and there were always sets to check in open areas that required the use of hip-boots. My knees still feel sore from the many hours of kneeling on the ice next to 'rat houses. It was and still is a tough way to harvest muskrat fur, but the quality of the fur is amazing. We also learned the magic of Conibears used under the ice when there was clear ice to use to find the runs. The way the muskrats run under the first ice is phenomenal. They are fearless with the protection of the ice and can be seen swimming under the ice at all times of the day. Traps could be set and run constantly under these conditions and catches made instantly after setting the trap. All it took was an ice chisel, long gloves, and Conibears of the 110 size. Of course the days of clear ice in Minnesota are usually very few, as snow usually covers the sloughs and lakes quickly after the ice forms.

I remember those steel-wool skies that spit frozen chunks of winter at me as I tended traps. I learned in those formative years that the weather meant so much to our success. We learned to hit the open water hard and set as many traps as possible, for the easy days of open water trapping seldom lasted. We looked for the signs of clear, calm, nights with sunsets ablaze in the dust of harvest, to assure us of another fair day. We knew that the wisps of mare's tails drifting across the sky would soon change the weather to wet and finally to cold. When the wind blew from the east and storm clouds mounded in the west, we knew that the frenzied feeding runs of the mink would bring the greatest numbers of them past our sets. Even if the snow piled deep, we would dig some big bucks out from under the slush and snow on the next check.

The weather was always our best friend and our greatest enemy. It always dictated what we did, always called the shots. Sometimes we'd set up a big 'rat slough by boat and have it freeze up, forcing us to break the boat through a half inch of ice to each set. Other times we'd set a slough on the first good walking ice, only to have a thaw set in leaving us unable to get to the sets on the ice. The weather taught us to move like crazy when conditions were right and it taught us to be patient duringt unworkable times of storms and severe cold snaps. Nuances of weather, climate, and the changing seasons became clear to us. The importance of such things as setting locations that caught the low-profile rays of the late fall sun to thaw these locations during the day became second nature. We learned about windswept locations, when dirt trapping, that stayed clear of deep snow and produced fox later in the season. The weather forced us to prioritize our assault, knowing that the very shallow ponds should be trapped first since they would be the first to freeze up. The spring holes could be saved as good locations to work when other water froze.

We trapped a lot of lakes and marshes. I remember one lake we trapped was also used as a winter site for ice-racing. People would bring old cars out when the ice was thick enough and race them around the lake. Inevitably some cars would die out there never to be driven again. I guess there was no one around to make sure that the cars were all cleared off the ice before spring, so lots of cars were left to sink as the ice left in spring. When we trapped the lake in the fall, muskrats would be using the old car bodies left near the shore as places to feed or build their houses. A typical day would hold conversations like:

"How did the sets on the old forty-two Ford produce?"

"The set on the passenger side held a nice 'rat. The trap on the right fender was sprung and the set on the trunk was untouched."

I remember one season when we got the rights to trap a well-populated muskrat marsh. We agreed to pay the landowner ten cents for every 'rat we took from his property. It was a pretty fair price since muskrats were selling for about a dollar each at the time. The marsh was dotted with houses and feed beds. We went to scout the marsh at dusk before the season opened and watched the muskrats swim and feed. The numbers were incredible. It was a place we really wanted to set up before the water froze. We decided to split up on the opening day. We had another good lake that we usually trapped, and we decided that my brother would drop me and a bunch of traps at the lake so I could set up that area. He took the truck with our duck boat and went over to the marsh we had leased so he could set it up. We both set traps all day and by evening the muskrats were beginning to come out. I started checking sets, since a lot of my sets were Conibears set at den entrances. Towards sunset I began taking muskrats out of traps and by the time he picked me up I had already taken twenty-one 'rats. I was feeling pretty good about that. I then looked into the back of the truck and saw his pile of muskrats. He had taken forty-seven 'rats from the sets he had made in the marsh. I don't think the landowner made much of a profit on the deal, but we felt we did well after we had trapped that marsh for a few days. He was happy to get some income from a piece of property that produced no crops and was basically worthless to him otherwise. The population of muskrats was so large in the marsh that they had dug almost every bit of vegetation out of the shoreline and bottom of that body of water. Interestingly, it had always been a very densely vegetated marsh, but the muskrats completely changed that environment. Had we not trapped most of the 'rats from the slough, they would have surely starved in great numbers during the coming winter. The reeds never returned to that marsh for many years and the population of muskrats has never returned to the levels of that season.

Chapter 4

"Flat-Tail Days"

WHEN WE WERE GROWING UP, trapping was a fall and winter activity. As I grew into my teens, a new dimension of trapping and an entirely new season began to emerge. Beaver were relatively rare in the sixties in southern Minnesota, but a few would pop up on occasion. The season then, was a spring season, which began in March and extended into late April. There was a ten-beaver limit—when you bought a license you were issued ten steel, locking tags that had to be put on the beaver at the site of taking them. The law specifically told you to insert the tag into the mouth and it had to come out the eye hole. I guess it was to ensure that no one upgraded to larger beaver to make the ten count limit worth more money. There could be no sorting. Once you put your tag on a beaver it was included in the limit with no possibility of getting a better one later. It is really amazing how the beaver population has revived in recent years and now beaver are more likely than not to be considered a nuisance. There are no limits on beaver and many townships in Minnesota now even pay a bounty on the industrious rascals.

Tracks in the Mud

    Back in the sixties beavers were an amazing and almost exotic species for me to pursue. They had the aura of the old mountain men and I dreamed of catching them. I read all about beaver trapping and finally found a colony I could trap. I bought my license and set out with my ice chisel, wire, a couple of number four long-spring traps, snowshoes, pack-basket, and all the other tools of the trade I had read I would need. I also had invested in a 330 Conibear that proved to be a great asset. The luck of that first season was that the March opening actually found the weather warm enough that the beavers were coming out from under the ice at the flowing water on the dam. There were some great set possibilities, and I made three good sets including a den set under the ice.

    My first check was a Sunday morning before church. Taking into consideration the long walk to the colony and the gear required to do the check I started out early. That first foray into beaver trapping proved that one can learn to do things by just reading about them. Those three traps were the first I had ever attempted to set for beavers. Long story short, beginner's luck definitely on my side, I had two blankets (beaver categorized in the largest size grade) and a yearling on the first check. I had somehow done what most trappers try to do upon setting up a new colony: take the two adult beaver and some of the one-year-old animals. It was about a hundred fifty pounds of beaver that I had to cart out in one trip in order to make it back in time for church. It was a long but very excited walk.

    Trapping beaver was much like trapping big muskrats. The similarity ended when I started skinning and stretching the beavers. I soon learned that the real work started when one began handling the pelts. Fleshing and stretching beaver took considerably longer than trapping them. I think I came close to filling my tags that year. There were many long hikes to the Minnesota River where I made scent and bait sets that produced beaver that were traveling up and down the river. There were a few other spots where I found signs and was able to connect on a flat-tail or two. Seeing those oval-

A couple of hefty "blanket" beaver from the 1960s.

shaped pelts hung on the garage walls was a thrilling sight for me, linking me again to the old mountain men who pursued beaver long ago.

When the trapping was done, the selling of pelts began. My education on the beaver business had only begun as I trapped and put the pelts up on stretching boards. Selling was where I really got an education. Selling muskrat and mink fur was a relatively easy and simple process. Beaver on the other hand enlightened me on the whole subject of grading fur, and I soon found that there are a lot of either real, or in some cases, fabricated grades. I soon learned about "rubbed" and "singed" and "bleached" and "flat" and "springy" and a whole host of possible defects that can keep one from getting top dollar for a beaver skin. I also learned that no two fur buyers will grade the same and that shopping around can pay dividends. Of course the basic grade was for size and that was determined by adding the length and width of the open-stretched pelt. If the two measurements add up to sixty-five inches or more, the beaver was considered a "blanket," which is the pricing basis. Five-inch breaks separate the various sizes and, of course, the price drops with each drop in size. I found that various fur buyers would come up with different measurements depending upon how they did the measurement. Some went nose to tail, others went from the eyes to the tail, some cross measured, and others docked if the pelt wasn't perfectly round in the way it was stretched. Selling beaver taught me a lot about subjectivity and business in general.

Spring beaver season became a regular tradition for us and we began to take some trips up to northern Minnesota, which was the real beaver country back then. The lakes and streams are of course countless and beavers are present in most places. We trapped the Aitkin area and ventured up to Grand Rapids and Park Rapids and other points in between.

One particular season we were trapping in the Aitkin area. It was late in the season and the streams were totally open and there was very little snow left. I can still smell the smoke in the air because it was a dry spring and there were actually fires burning somewhere. I remember setting a 330 Conibear in a narrow spot between two beaver dams on a stream. As I traveled down to the next location and began setting another trap I heard a huge splash back where I had just set the Conibear. Going back to the location I found a just-caught beaver dead in the trap. The beaver really become active during those spring days when they have just been freed from their icy prison of the ending winter season.

We had quite a camping outfit back then. My dad had built a fish house that fit into the back of a standard pickup truck. It was built in a "T" fashion so there was a bunk on each side of the fish house that hung over either side of the truck. There was a propane stove for heat and a cookstove as well as a gas light. We had the heavily insulated shelter turn-buckled down to the sides of an old sixty Chevrolet pickup. We hauled that makeshift camper on many trapping excursions into the northern woods. I recall one time when the transmission was going out in the old truck and the only way we could keep it from popping out of third gear when we were going down the highway was to hang a heavy lunch pail on the shift lever.

The old fish house was built to keep us warm in sub-zero weather, which meant that it wasn't built all that light due to the materials available at that time. The six-cylinder engine labored to move the rig along. One day in early April the snow drifts were melting in the mixed aspen and pine woods of northern Minnesota. The sky was as blue as it could get and the woods were still, permeated only by the drumming of ruffed grouse and the trickle of water running in its pursuit of lower ground. The map we had showed a small creek deep in those

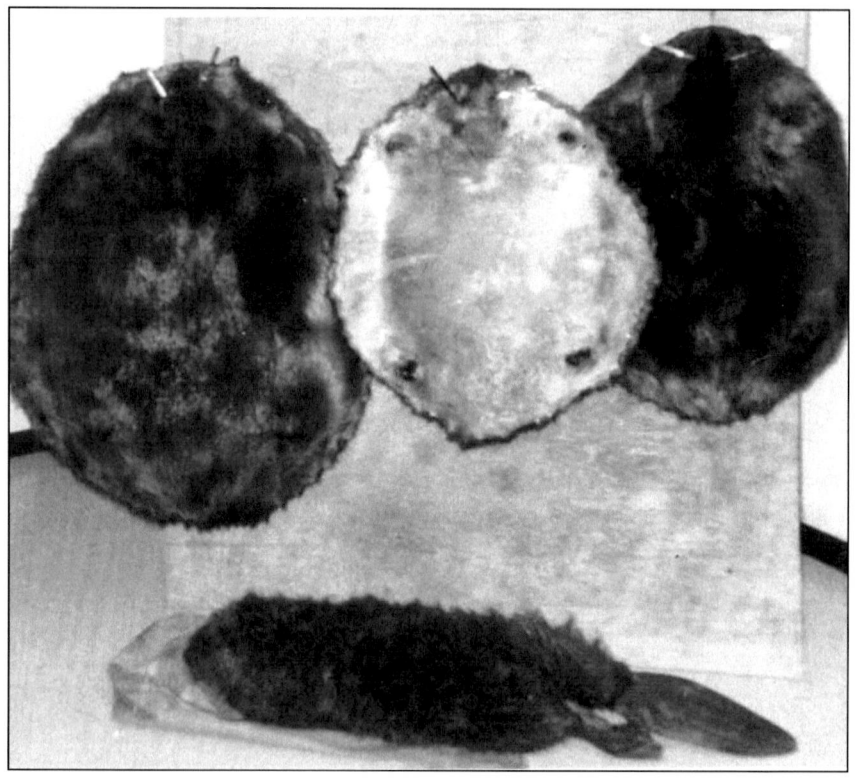
Stretched and dried beaver pelts with the metal locking tags from the 1960s.

woods with the dotted line of an old logging trail leading almost to the stream. The stream seemed like a shoe-in for having a good beaver population. We knew the beaver were coming out of most of the dams, and accessing the stream would likely provide some good sets. The logging trail began as a pretty good two-track, with little snow in the ruts and pretty solid footing. We decided to drive at least as far as we could to save some heavy packing on foot. Of course the old pickup was two-wheel drive, since we had hardly even heard of four-by-fours back then. We started down the trail wondering why no other trappers had apparently driven down to the stream before us. The trail began to drop slightly, which seemed only normal as one traveled toward a stream.

The trees seemed to close a bit nearer to both sides of the trail as we progressed. Soon the ruts got deeper and water and ice lay in the bottom of the tracks. There was nowhere to park or turn around. Each low spot contained deep ruts that caused the burdened old truck to groan and grind in first gear to negotiate the difficult spot.

We began to worry that in the next area of deep ruts we would bottom out and hang up. Of course there were no cell phones back then, not that one would have service in that area even today.

Author with prime spring beaver pelts from the late 1960s.

Tracks in the Mud

We were far from any blacktop road and even farther from any town. All we could do now was to stay in the ruts and hope for a place to turn around. Often I have seen old rusted vehicle bodies out in these woods and I began to picture our old red Chevy covered with vines with a fish house rotting on her back. Finally we found a place to turn off and turn around and then wondered if the truck would have the power to carry us back up that hill.

As I recall we checked out the stream and I presume we walked the trail on subsequent visits. We did get back out from the lowlands and parked at the trail head, to camp for the night. Spring beaver trapping definitely had its moments, but that time of year was a gorgeous time to spend in the woods. Of course there were always the spring snows and cold fronts that slowed the breakup, but the weather generally got better in the spring rather than steadily worse as it did in the fall. To me the exploration of new trapping spots was always a thrill. Following streams was an addiction and going just another curve or just another clump of aspens was hard to stop. I suspect it was probably me who insisted we venture down that deeply rutted logging trail. Sometimes we would be rewarded with a great spot to trap, but other times we would be tired and disappointed at the end of the excursion. Fortunately my more practical brother tempered my unbridled optimism with a little common sense or we would probably still be wandering around in some willow swamp, lost to the ages.

Although beaver had a pretty good price compared to other furs at the time, the extremely hard work and long days associated with their capture took most of the profit out of the pursuit. I did see that some money could be made at trapping, even though fur prices were still mainly pretty depressed. There usually seemed to be plenty of competition at beaver trapping in the northern part of the state. There had always been some beaver to be found in that region and there was a pretty strong beaver-trapping tradition in those areas. The thirty or forty dollars that a blanket beaver brought during the sixties was a nice chunk of money back then with gas prices pretty cheap and wages much lower than now, however there still was a limit on beaver so you couldn't trap large numbers. Of course in the remote areas of northern Minnesota, where both money and jobs were scarce every one in the family of a trapper probably got a license which increased the number of beaver a family could market. To me a true fur boom had to include high prices on species that were abundant and could be trapped in numbers. Those days were on the horizon, but we had no way of knowing that as we plodded along with dollar 'rats and five-dollar fox.

As snowmobiles came into common use, the fox quickly learned that snowmobiles meant danger and they didn't lie out in the open. People riding snowmobiles would come upon a fox and give chase. In deep snow a fox could be run down with a snowmobile. I think the genetics for laying on snow banks quickly became eliminated for the species.

In the pre-snowmobile days, fox could be hunted on cold sunny days. They slept outside in a location exposed to the sun. Using a good center-fire varmint rifle with an accurate range of three-hundred yards, an approach could often be made on a sleeping fox and it could be shot right in its bed. I bought a used .222 Remington with a six-power scope and was amazed at its accuracy. With a pair of snowshoes and a set of binoculars I figured I could spend some enjoyable days of spot-and-stalk fox hunting.

If the wind was right a hunter could even sneak close enough to shoot foxes with a shot gun. After I got my first predator call, we just set up a ways from the sleeping fox and called. Very often a curious fox came right into shotgun range.

Chapter 5

"A B.A. and a Ph.D. While Packing Heat in the Dorm"

AS WE HIT THE LATE SIXTIES and I went off to college, the fox trapping bug hit us pretty hard. There were lots of red foxes and permission was pretty easy to obtain, as most farmers had little time for predators that ate chickens and killed game-birds. These were the days of some pretty incredible fox catches by long-liners who knew the mystery of the dirt hole set. I can remember pictures of several hundred fox pelts tacked to a barn printed in the local newspaper. Soon, most pastures and fence crossings had worn circles in the black soil by the first part of November, where fox had been taken. Dirt trapping became the icon of the long-liner. Orange eyes shining in the headlights of the old truck became the ritual of early mornings. We learned how most creatures were attracted to holes in the soil and fresh dirt. Soon the smell of skunk musk in the night made me think immediately of fox trapping. Skunks were of course the double-edged blade of fox trapping. They had to be dealt with but also portended future fox catches as their scent was a great call lure for all foxes.

We learned to hit the fox on the warm dirt of late October, no antifreeze needed, just lots of sets and dry weather. Fox could be mass-caught in these conditions. We learned to gang sets, that is set several sets in a good location and make multiple catches. This was our college education in trapping and it seemed to coincide with my college education in general. We still went to the water when the mink and muskrat season opened, but the dirt changed our lives as trappers, because we now were multi-dimensional trappers. We did dry sets and water sets covering more species in our territory. I really began to realize that great numbers of fur could be taken on a long auto line. A system began to emerge that could only be enhanced by higher fur prices. Soon the dreams of kids like me would be within reach, dreams that seemed almost stupid a few years earlier.

We had no inkling of the world economics that would influence our humble trade. We only knew the cold crisp mornings of excited anticipation. We only looked ahead to the next set and the glow of mink eyes in the beam of a flashlight or longed for the jumping form of a red fox as we topped a green-pastured hill.

The fascination of the quarry never ebbed. Each day on the trap line taught new horizons, each track in the snow led to new realizations. All this was only a training ground. We were among ground-floor participants in what would become the greatest fur boom in history. Many would come late and try to mimic the trends, but they would only flicker briefly and then go off to other endeavors.

Now the land began to pour itself out to me. I began to look at every landscape I passed from a trapper's perspective. Each field edge, each stream, each inside or outside turn in the course of a stream told me a tale of what fur ran there, how each species would react to that bit of real estate. Every fence, every hill, and every field-road told me a tale; read like a book.

Tracks in the Mud

I learned to stop at every crossing on every dirt road and pick up on tracks, droppings, even hairs caught on barbed-wire fences. This was ground-floor knowledge of a world-wide industry. This was the raw material of exports and fortunes made and lost. I was only a kid who needed to know why a mink ran a certain side of a stream, or why a muskrat decided to dig a burrow in a certain location on a lake shore. Yet kids like me all across the continent fueled an incredible gold rush of sorts. I couldn't know that laws would be rewritten, rural wars would be fought over those very stream-banks and lakeshores, and some outdoorsmen would even be propelled toward wealth.

The late sixties and early seventies were a pivotal time in Minnesota for trapping. We still had the old long-line mink trappers that had always been operating here, but a new young generation of trappers was also emerging. Encouraged by higher fur prices and easier access to the methods of trapping, brought on by publications and how-to books, these folks were beginning to impact the trade. Access to private land became tighter, because many rural kids were again trapping, and more folks were taking time to spend trapping again in the fall and winter. The boom had begun. It seems to have begun a bit earlier in the northern states like Minnesota. We had naturally a better grade of fur than states farther south and a deeper tradition for the trade. Trapping areas were much coveted, and there were few places to expand without encroaching upon someone else's trapping territory. As my own life changed, I soon found there were still places to get ahead of the curve in the trapping game.

Around 1970, there were war protest marches, hippies, and LSD, old norms and rules were being questioned, and the world was rocketing to the moon. Going to college in the big city of St. Paul, Minnesota, was an adjustment for a person used to getting up on

November mornings and checking traps. It was indeed a changing world, but I guess I wasn't ready to allow it to change me. Soon the back of my pickup came back to campus from home with a few essentials. Traps, stakes, hip boots, and other tools of the trade. I didn't know exactly where I would set traps in this area, but I did know that, in Minnesota, one is never too far from lakes and streams. Soon I had a trap line established out from the suburbs, and I even found some 'rat trapping on some city lakes, which, as far as I could determine, weren't closed to trapping. Believe it or not a .22 rifle found its way under my bed in the dorm, and no one seemed to have the least bit of fear of someone carrying a cased gun into the dorm. How times have changed. Now, such an attempt would land a student in jail.

Weekends and holidays were still spent trapping near our home but the city line kept the trapping fever at bay during the week. Trapping was still a hobby and no great amounts of money were generated on the trap line. It was a source of extra money for one going to college, but no road to riches. At that time there always were some fox trapping weekends before the water season. Then the mink and muskrat season kicked in and ran in earnest through Thanksgiving vacation. Fox trapping began anew as winter set in, and Christmas vacation was a combination of fox and ice trapping for muskrats.

March was the beginning of beaver season, and spring break and Easter vacation were anticipated for spring beaver trapping. Somehow classes got taken, papers got written, and a degree was earned. Since I was pursuing a teaching degree, I had to schedule student teaching and other in-field experiences. I fit in student teaching during winter quarter, where I missed the least amount of opportunity for running a trap line in that time slot. I still remember having to do a child study for one of my child psychology classes. I decided to do the study on one of my older cousin's young boys. My cousin too was a trapping enthusiast, and I think I spent most of my observation time talking about sets, water-proof trap coverings, and fur prices.

During those school years, I worked on a grounds maintenance crew at a golf course. Some of my best duties there were trapping the burrowing muskrats out of the water hazards and, of course, helping to exterminate some of the thousands of ground squirrels from the course. Besides working, summers were also great for scouting out the fur population. I began to learn how important it was to prospect areas, and be on top of the best areas when the season opened. The scouting and the anticipation of the season became almost as much fun as the actual trapping season. Other outdoor pursuits such as fishing and hunting were also good opportunities to check out the fur numbers in an area.

My wife-to-be, was also getting her degree in education. Amazingly, my insane love of the outdoors didn't seem to bother her. In fact, I think it intrigued her. At least she ended up marrying me. I soon would get my Ph.D. in trapping, and as we started our married life, things indeed got piled higher and deeper in terms of trapping equipment, fur, and at times even carcasses. My wife has always supported me in my trapping endeavors, and it makes all the difference when one is involved in such a demanding trade.

Chapter 6
"Wading into a Cornhusker Classroom"

WHEN I GRADUATED FROM COLLEGE, I assumed that I would probably teach in a school in Minnesota, preferably in a rural area. Soon I realized that I was graduating during a time when teaching jobs were not extremely plentiful. I received a placement in, of all places, Nebraska. I had planned to buy a new canoe and plenty of water trapping equipment to continue pursuing my trapping in Minnesota. Now those ideas had to be put on hold. Nebraska seemed like a long way from Minnesota, and I envisioned a flat, dry, treeless plain where no trapping could possibly take place. Yet, I was indeed lucky to even have a teaching job since they were scarce. So off I went to Nebraska, leaving all the lakes and marshes of Minnesota behind and anticipating a place where little fur lived.

Still, one of the first things I did was to get a copy of the hunting and trapping regulations from Nebraska. My first impression was how wide open and liberal the regulations were as compared to Minnesota's trapping laws. The seasons ran basically from the first part of November until the end of March. Pretty much everything was open and most traps and methods were legal. There were no restrictions against multiple-catch traps, and no trap tags were required. There were no restrictions on hours of operation, making night trapping legal. Leaving the deep traditions of trapping in Minnesota for the plains of Nebraska was indeed a change. Trapping during the early seventies was at a very immature stage in Nebraska. There were few trappers and they didn't get much attention from the rural population or from the Nebraska Game and Parks Commission. Don't get me wrong, there were some long-liners who had discovered Nebraska for the great fur-producing area that it is, but the main population had not yet found out what really was out there. I knew that Craig O'Gorman trapped Nebraska during some of those years before he moved to Montana and some of the local guys like Don Bolte out of Beaver Crossing put up incredible numbers of 'coon.

  But the local fur buyers paid very low prices to the local trappers, and there was not a great deal of enthusiasm for trapping in general. The main fur-buying line most trappers received as they sold fur was that the quality of Nebraska fur was inferior to that of areas farther north. Therefore, it was worth less money. That began to change as the world hungered for more volume of fur and buying became more competitive in Nebraska. I also soon discovered that Nebraska had more miles of waterways than any other state. I had grown up as a lake and marsh trapper with little knowledge of stream trapping. Most of the streams and drainage ditches in Minnesota were controlled by the old-time traditional "bridge trappers," and guys like me found little opportunity to break into that deal, which was primarily mink trapping. I didn't know it at the time, but Nebraska was long-hair fur country, and we were entering an incredible period of the resurgence of interest in long-haired furs.

Growing up in an era of mink and muskrat trapping with long-haired furs such as fox and raccoon being almost worthless, I was still in a water-trapping mode. My baptism into stream and coyote trapping would soon begin. Fortunately I thought of coyotes as just big foxes and had a good starting point for trapping them. When I left Minnesota for Nebraska, there were few coyotes to speak of in southern Minnesota. Fox were plentiful, but the coyote invasion had not yet begun. Nebraska on the other hand was the perfect inversion of the canine population of southern and western Minnesota with most of the canine predators being coyotes, with just a few pockets of fox in areas where the coyotes had not driven them completely out of the vicinity.

So the trapper-teacher arrived in Nebraska. I was excited to be teaching science. Of course biology was my great interest but as an elementary teacher I taught all branches of science. The kids were great and my interest in the outdoors made for a good connection with those kids. They really wanted to know about wildlife and how it connects to us. I had the opportunity to refute some of the misconceptions about hunters and trappers. What other elementary science program could kids get the chance to dissect large mammals and see the wonder of the internal systems until a trained teacher was able to provide the opportunity? Of course now most schools would shut down such a learning experience, citing some kind of health rules or maybe even some cruelty reasons to not allow it to take place. Fortunately, the principle I worked with believed in having kids learn from first-hand experience as much as possible. My students were totally excited by science and the "hands on" experience was unforgettable. Girls, who later might be convinced by peer pressure in junior high school that cutting open a beaver was "gross," embraced the awesome mystery in elementary school and grew up with a true appreciation of biology. I hoped a lot of my fifth and sixth grade classes graduated many future medical students who also had a love for the outdoors and did not write off consumptive use of resources as inherently bad. I am thankful for a principal who was accepting of a teacher who sometimes was found in his classroom late at night correcting papers while wearing hip-boots, probably with a puddle of muddy water around his feet. I may have left the school as early as possible at times, but I did return to get my work done. I digress into the joy of teaching kids because we trappers are all just kids at heart, and we have not lost the joy of learning. Each day in the classroom of the outdoors inspired me with awe and wonder. Each day on the trap line was a day of learning. I entered the classroom of the outdoors of Nebraska ready to learn.

  Like I said, Nebraska is Minnesota upside down. At first I couldn't figure out why it seemed so different, and then it dawned on me that there were no trees on the top of the hills, only in the stream valleys. Folks told me that Nebraska was so beautiful because there weren't any trees and mountains to get in the way of the scenery. In Minnesota we tended to have trees on the tops of hills as well as in the valleys. There were very few marshes in eastern Nebraska. Instead I found many farm ponds created by earth dams. They came in all sizes and shapes. They all had a deep end near the dam and usually had a bit of shallow often marshy wetland on the end where the water flowed into the impoundment. There were also many man-made lakes of pretty good size. Some were open to trapping, while others required a special permit obtained by a special lottery drawing.

  It was exciting to get the feel for a new landscape, new regulations, and new types of habitat. Many things were the same, however, such as the sign, the tracks, and the places where the furbearers traveled. Other things were new—the deep muddy streams, the big fields of milo and wheat, the farm ponds, and the incredible weather shifts, which were even more abrupt than those in Minnesota.

I arrived in Nebraska during late summer. Finding a place to rent was a priority and of course it had to be a place which would accommodate my outdoor activities. I was lucky enough to find a place where I had the main floor of a house and also had use of part of the basement and the garage. I had room for my trapping and hunting gear.

When I left Minnesota with all of my hunting and trapping stuff, I was told by many that I was crazy to even take it, because there would be no place to use the equipment. I set out to prove them wrong. Almost immediately I began forays into the rural countryside. Few places are more rural than Nebraska. I got an overview of the area near where I lived and used maps to find streams, reservoirs, and other features that would indicate furbearers' presence. It was like a new and blank canvas. I had no conception of competition, no biases about landowners, and nothing to lose by pursuing a route for a trap line. The land was almost all privately owned, and getting to know farmers and ranchers was absolutely a must. I soon discovered the greatest resource in the state of Nebraska was its people. I had time to knock on doors well before the season. Although most landowners were a bit skeptical of strangers, they were always friendly and ready to visit and get to know me. I was truly interested in the land and the crops and the wildlife. I learned much from the landowners and I also soon found out they had little problem with someone who would rid their stock pond dams of burrowing muskrats, their streams of 'coons, and their range of coyotes.

I soon found that I was truly in on the ground floor of trapping this vast prairie land. Most people hadn't really been asked permission to trap, and I found that the upward trend in fur prices hadn't really affected the area much to this point. I keyed in on the very best farms, the ones situated in the good stream-bottom areas. I spent most of my free time knocking on doors and asking permission. I kept meticulous notes on each place and also soon found that most farmers and ranchers owned or controlled much more land than the average farmer in Minnesota at the time. Usually if I asked for permission to trap a particular area I found that the landowner also had many more parcels of land. Often the farmer would say something like, "If you want to trap some coyotes you sure could get some on such and such farm a mile down the road . . ." and then he would give me directions to another quarter section of his land. Often conversations were long, and soon many of these farmers became friends, who over the years that I spent in Nebraska looked forward to my visits and a chance to talk. Some even invited me over for dinner and really appreciated not only my trapping and predator control but also really appreciated someone who respected their land and their rights as landowners.

In Nebraska I learned the intricate connection of the land and its inhabitants. I began to see the land as a funnel for various furbearers. Its contours and prominences were the driving force for all travel by the furbearers there. Watersheds became a book to read and crop rotations started to have real meaning for me. I learned how the harvests and the crops affected things like the dispersion of coyote and fox families. As the crops came out and raptor numbers peaked, causing rodents to be consumed in great numbers, canine predators needed to disperse from their whelping areas to larger ranges. Places where multiple catches of the year's pups could be made early in the season, soon would hold less predators, whether the area was trapped or not. Areas that had many great locations in the early season soon only had a few good crossing locations where most traveling canines moved through the area.

One of the great things I came to appreciate in Nebraska was the length of the seasons at the time. It allowed me to get a great cross-section of furbearer habits and what they did during different times. The long raccoon season, for example, taught me how the early season is dictated much by crops and food sources in the fields, and later as the crops came out and the streams began to freeze, the 'coons began to feed in the spring holes where the water stayed open and the crayfish were still available. I also suspected that the water was warmer than the air and thus these spring holes were a comfortable place to hunt.

I learned a great deal about land trapping of canines. It started with the easy, warm weather of late October and early November, when no anti-freeze was needed to keep dirt sets working and the young of the year were easy pickings. Later, I would need to cover more ground, and the December weather necessitated carrying dry dirt and anti-freeze for dirt sets. I learned that the effectiveness of the dirt sets was still great even when snow covered the ground. Finally, I really broadened my horizons as I learned the art of snaring. Now I had a tool that worked even when the snow got deep and the ground was frozen so deep that it was very hard to dig sets and pound stakes. Snaring taught me a new way to think like a coyote. It taught me to put a noose in an exact spot to catch a coyote. Really, every snare set was a type of trail set, even if there was an attractor in the area. Soon I adapted my snaring knowledge to 'coon trapping, and it added to my 'coon catch as well. One had to think about an animal's anatomy and its distinct little habits that helped put them into the noose.

My first years in Nebraska were my time of graduation from secondary trapping to the college level. The great diversity of fur and the length of the seasons opened many new areas. For the first time I learned of spring trapping for muskrats. That had been only something I heard my dad talk about. Apparently there had been spring seasons in Minnesota many years back. In Nebraska the season extended from November until March, and, therefore, afforded a chance at break-up trapping.

Since there is a lot of dry land in Nebraska, land trapping became a larger part of the trapping experience. Here, I also ran into some legendary predator trappers. Craig O'Gorman ran lines in Nebraska. A guy named Ivan White trapped in the Sand Hills and lots of other great coyote trappers ran in the Sand Hills catching the legendary light-colored and, at the time, valuable silky coyotes of that area. There were also some incredible raccoon trappers, and they piled up some of the most amazing catches on the many waterways of the Cornhusker State. I remember a guy from Beaver Crossing named Don Bolte who also was a fur buyer. He showed up in a very wide area of central and eastern Nebraska. There are always rumors of fur catches in the trapping circles and the rumors of his catches went way into the four figure area per season. As my lines grew, I crossed paths with a lot of great trappers, learning from them and also finding them to be mostly very hard-working and efficient operators. This is the area in which I really grew in my education. Efficiency and hard work were key concepts in trapping as in any other endeavor. Some of the lessons learned during these years were instrumental in later success in other businesses. Mapping, organization, and pre-planning became a larger part of trapping than the actual taking of the fur. Scheduling to optimize the weather, trapping laws, and competition was an absolute "must" to be as successful as was possible.

I soon realized that I was into a good thing in Nebraska. There was less competition, lots of places to trap and lots of fur.

Amazingly, the common furs like raccoon, coyotes, and muskrats were coming into great favor in the marketplace. These species were abundant in my newly adopted state and I was young and ready to tap the resource. I didn't know immediately how it would all play out, but the excitement of pretty decent prices and long seasons was great. Of course a young teacher in those years, in a small parochial school like the one I taught in, earned less than six thousand dollars a year. Some extra trapping income would be very helpful. The incentives were as great as the excitement of the trap line.

I'm always amazed at the perfect storm which brought things together in the seventies for the fur harvesters in America. Obviously lots of kids like me had grown up in rural areas and had learned to trap as youngsters. Some of us were more than a little intrigued with the concept of professional fur trapping. There were many years of on-the-job training where fur prices weren't great, but that left lots of areas to trap and learn the trade. As prices began to increase, we were able to build knowledge and equipment, as well as relationships with landowners. The almost unreal coincidence of both long- and short-haired furs becoming popular at the same time opened up the possibility of running multiple species and being profitable during a longer time frame in a given season. Having the common farmland furbearers at good prices gave easy access to the fur industry and encouraged people to cover incredible amounts of land and rack up large catches. The other important factor during these years was the great volume of wild fur that the world-wide markets were able to absorb. Fur was being used a great deal, not only in the United States but also in foreign countries. Fur buyers were able to move vast quantities of fur and little carry-over each season meant that they had the money and the speculative incentive to buy the new fur crop each year. Long-lining and even state-hopping came into its own during the seventies. For me there was a long ways to go before I was to realize my ultimate goal of full-time trapping.

My first season in Nebraska was a part-time endeavor. I guess I should qualify that with saying that to some, getting up at three in the morning to check traps and then going back out after school until after dark is more than part-time work. There was also the preparation involved with being a full-time teacher, which I did take seriously. One of the big legal changes for me was the lack of trapping hours. In Minnesota trappers had been restricted in those years to a 6:00 a.m. to 6:00 p.m. trapping day. In Nebraska it was a twenty-four-hour proposition. That meant the season opened at minight, a fact I used to great advantage in later years when the competition became great. That year the season opened on November fifteenth and it happened to be a Wednesday. I don't think a board of education ever had a teacher request the first day of trapping season off before, but I convinced them to allow it. I think I had to pay a sub, but felt it was well worth the money. I headed out in the wee hours of that first morning and set up some public lakes. I slapped in a lot of sets the first day and tied up some nice areas to trap. I always anticipated the weekends when I could re-group my trap line and extend to new areas.

There was also the matter of becoming engaged to be married. That fall was a very busy and changing time in my life. My wife was then, and still is, the most wonderfully supportive person imaginable when it comes to all my outdoor endeavors. I think she knew what she was getting into when she agreed to marry me, but being an understanding and adaptable person certainly helped.

Chapter 7

"Adopting a State and Engaging a Wife"

I TRAPPED ALONE THE FIRST YEAR in the Cornhusker state and actually continued the tradition as long as I trapped there. My wife did accompany me at times, which was always a lot of fun. Trapping with some one else was a great joy and my times trapping with my brother and later with my son are some of the most memorable times on the trap line, but I learned to work very efficiently alone as well. I always felt that taking on a trapping partner was almost as serious as marriage. They must be able to work together and really complement each other. I kind of got into a routine of trapping alone and learned to enjoy the solitude and complete freedom of running solo. There were never any excuses if things didn't go as planned. I learned to double-check myself and take responsibility for everything. This was a good precursor for other businesses I later pursued.

I learned a lot that first season. I learned about the weather, which is extremely variable in Nebraska. I learned volumes about stream trapping. I learned about fluctuating water levels, which were never a problem on the marshes and lakes of Minnesota. I found the slick mud banks of the streams in Nebraska to be both good and bad. They were great for holding and drowning 'coon but were sometimes a challenge to negotiate. The incredible racoon numbers here were new to me, and the ease with which one could force them into traps on the steep banks was really fun. I learned more about raccoon trapping than anything else. Being always strapped for time, I really learned to cover my area by trapping bridges and other road right-of-way areas. The best crossings and best locations began to become evident.

The best thing about my first season trapping in Nebraska was that there was little competition and I was able to get my education without too much harassment. Of course I looked for and prized the mink that ran those streams. Nebraska had large mink but they were a much lighter brown color than specimens I was used to in Minnesota. I set for them and learned to catch them despite all the raccoon also found along the streams. It would not be long before I would be setting mainly for raccoon and only taking the mink as a secondary catch. As 'coon prices began to soar, going after the less abundant mink paled. My first season, I didn't trap until the season opened for mink and muskrat, although it was legal to trap raccoon earlier than the fifteenth of November, even with water sets. The new concept I began to learn was to take the 'coon and avoid the mink and muskrats. I would later become very good at not-catching mink and 'rats, so I could take the already prime raccoon that were abundant and valuable.

I took my first coyotes that first season in Nebraska. Coming from the fox-rich farmland of Minnesota, I started out treating coyotes just as if they were large fox. It really wasn't a bad beginning premise. I started out with some number one-and-a-half and number two coil-spring traps that had worked well for taking red fox. I pounded in the quarter-inch re-rod stakes that had held fox easily for me. I had no trouble catching the coyotes, but soon learned they were much more than over-sized foxes. I realized their great strength when I found the jaws literally pulled out of some of my traps. I also found that they were the masters at jacking stakes out of the ground. Fortunately, one of my students had a dad who was a great welder, and I soon developed the equipment needed to catch and hold the incredibly strong coyote. I bought the proper traps and made certain the ends of the jaws were bent to make sure they couldn't be pulled out. I made stakes out of half-inch re-rod which were longer with swivels that could not slide down the stake, to prevent the coyote from jacking the stake out of the ground.

    Coyotes had the habit of pulling upward and that pulled stakes out when they were short-chained. I learned the trick of some Nebraska coyote trappers of using long chains to keep the critters from being able to pull up directly on the stake. I did see a few coyotes leave the trap location when I spooked them, and they were lying on my side of the stake. As they crossed the area with the long chain they just pulled right out of the trap as I approached.

    When I trapped fox, the best and most humane way to dispatch a live trapped fox was to tap it across the nose, and when the animal was down to hold its neck down and apply pressure to its heart to stop it. This procedure would quickly kill the fox. I tried the technique with the first coyote I trapped in Nebraska and immediately had a coyote clamped firmly to my boot. Those boots always leaked after that incident and his teeth came very close to my foot inside the boot. The bottom line was that coyotes were very powerful and not a bit docile. I couldn't treat them like big foxes in almost any way.

Tracks in the Mud

My days started at about three in the morning, when I went out to the trap line and drove by as many sets as possible before I had to get to school. Most of my sets were close enough to roads that I could shine a light across a field to see if a catch had been made. Catches were quickly removed from the sets and the set re-made. I soon developed a head-lantern system that enabled me to keep my hands free while re-making sets. I pinned a light to my cap with a cord leading to a large square battery in the pocket of my sweatshirt. I felt like a fur-killing machine. I used a twenty-two rifle to dispatch live racoons and could kill one, remove it from the trap, and re-set it in minutes. The pressure of a tight schedule taught me some pretty important lessons on efficiency. I remember being in a great hurry one morning and accidentally left my twenty-two rifle lying next to a bridge on a gravel road. When I realized I had left the gun, it was too late to go back and make it to school. I fretted over the gun all day and finally returned that evening and found it lying alongside the road right where I had left it. Either not much traffic used that road or no one had noticed the gun.

After a full day at school, I headed out to check more traps and set new areas. After checking all my traps, I'd skin and handle fur and correct papers for school. Of course there were also evening meetings sprinkled into the schedule along with cooking meals and other domestic stuff like washing clothes for teaching.

I remember the place I was renting had a basement that was split into two parts. Half of the basement was part of my apartment rental, and I of course used that area for handling my fur. The other half of the basement belonged to another apartment, which was rented out to a young couple. I don't think they appreciated me down in the basement at all hours of the night skinning critters and rattling fur stretchers. I don't think there was even any insulation between the apartment and my fur room. I did try to keep from skinning skunks down there, but I'm sure the aroma of a few mink did make it through to their place. They never complained, and I guess I was so busy I never got to know them very well. I got a few strange looks from them from time to time, and for some reason they never really made any great effort to get to know me either. I knew I would eventually have to get a place in the country, because no matter how discreet I was, some times it was hard to keep coyote carcasses from being noticed.

Besides the lessons learned about trapping the many streams and also the vast arena for coyote trapping, I also learned the power of the numerous stock ponds that dotted the countryside. They came in all sizes. Some were just watering holes for livestock and others were lakes complete with cabins and fish. They all had some things in common. They all had an earth dam where the water was deep and the bank was steep, with an overflow pipe to maintain a water level that wouldn't cause the dam to be destroyed in a big rain. They also all had a shallow end where typically reeds and other vegetation grew. These ponds were magnets for all sorts of furbearers. Raccoons hunted crawfish and other aquatic life along the dams and in the overflow water on the down stream side of the dam. Muskrats inhabited the ponds and mink came for the muskrats. Coyotes watered at the dams and hunted the other animals attracted to the water or the lush grass near the dams. Each stock pond offered many set possibilities. They were the mixed-bag capital of the trapping world. I soon had pocket sets along the steep banks, trail sets at the overflow pipe, dirt-hole sets for coyote on the dam itself, and many muskrat sets in the marshy end along with underwater dens along the pond shore.

Some of the larger ponds were places where great catches

could be made. It was essential to get permission on these, since they were all private ponds. Usually the landowners were happy to get the burrowing muskrats out of the ponds since they destroyed the earthen dams. The added fringe benefit of trapping these ponds was that the landowners would usually allow me to fish them as well. I caught some incredible bass and bluegills. I believe I was probably the first person to ice-fish many of them. Ice fishing wasn't very popular in Nebraska when I arrived. For a native Minnesotan like me it was natural. I remember catching a pail full of sixteen-ounce sunnies on one of these ponds one winter day. There was no limit on panfish at the time. Well the fishing is another story, just a sidelight to the trapping.

I also remember setting a number one-ten Conibear trap in a muskrat den on one of these ponds and upon pulling up the chain the next day I felt a weight much heavier than a muskrat in the trap. I pulled up a huge snapping turtle which had stuck his head into the muskrat den and got caught in the Conibear. I took him home and called a friend who had some experience with snapping turtle soup. We ate that big ugly critter. Just another fringe benefit of trapping, I guess.

Until that first year of trapping in Nebraska, I had used the number one-ten Conibear traps extensively for muskrats and mink and the large three-thirty Conibear for beaver. The mid-sized two-twenty was never of much interest. Here in Nebraska, where raccoon were a major target, I discovered the two-twenty Conibear was the perfect size. It eventually became my greatest tool in my 'coon arsenal. It killed the target quickly and humanely and always insured a quiet, dead catch when I ran the trap. It was very effective for a very busy trapper like me and assured the fur would still be there if I didn't check a set until later in the day.

Later the theft factor also became important. A dead racoon lying in the water attracted little attention, and he would be basically hidden until I came to collect him. Another thing I discovered while beaver trapping in den entrances and runs was that while a three-thirty was effective on beaver, it often missed the muskrats that swam in the same run. The two-twenty would not only catch the beaver if placed properly, but never missed muskrats that swam through. I soon decided that if I were only allowed one trap, it would be the two-twenty Conibear. It worked on every furbearer on my lines except coyote, and it might even have worked for them but there were just so many other good options, I never bothered to give it a try.

I encountered, quite quickly in my newly adopted state another furbearer that was never found on my trap lines in Minnesota. The opossum was a new and not totally welcome addition to my fur catch. Initially, they brought little money, but as long-haired fur grew in popularity, even the "grinners" paid their way. Sometimes, when trapping on dry land I just had to get through the abundant opossum crop before catching the racoons and coyotes. They added up and, as I recall during the best fur years, brought around five dollars, going a long way toward paying the gas bill. When I later moved back to Minnesota, I found that the opossum had moved into Minnesota as well and seems to have adapted to the colder climate.

The excitement of putting steel into a new state was great, even with the knowledge that I would have to learn to adapt to new conditions. The roads in Nebraska were a real challenge. In Minnesota most roads were graveled and posed little problem when they were wet. Snow of course could be troublesome, but the fall season was always one of accessible trap lines. Nebraska had lots of dirt roads. These were dusty in dry weather, but when it rained they became impassable. The fine-grained silt on these roads became like grease. They were so slick it was

Tracks in the Mud

nearly impossible to stay out of the ditches. When it rained, I soon learned that the only way to access sets along these roads was to hike. I did not have a four-wheel-drive truck at the time, but even that would not have made many of these roads passable. When the weather was dry, it was a dream, since there were roads on every mile and access was great. I also learned most landowners were fine with driving on their field roads, but gates must be positioned as found. Gates were a big issue in cattle country, and the trapper better make sure he was careful to keep closed gates closed and open gates open.

The weather was changeable in Nebraska, even more fickle than Minnesota. One of the first things someone told me when I got to Nebraska was, "If I didn't like the weather, I should just wait a minute and it would change." The first time I came to the state, I was greeted by one of the loudest and most violent thunderstorms I had ever experienced. Fronts swept across the Great Plains with amazing ferocity. Summer or winter, the weather could be violent. Wind was always a fact of life and precipitation levels could vary from so dry that log chains could be lost in the resulting cracks in the soil, to flooding rains that send creeks out of banks and make roads impossible to navigate. Even after growing up in Minnesota, I have to admit that some of the snowstorms in Nebraska were the worst I had ever seen. I recall one storm that packed the snow so tightly into my truck's engine compartment that the fan couldn't turn and the vehicle was dead until I meticulously cleaned the snow from the truck and dried it out completely. Fortunately a day later the sun came out, and the snow was melting.

The good thing about the changeable weather was that if it got cold, I could count on it warming up shortly, unlike some long winter stretches in Minnesota. Even in winter, the cold always abated and thaws came to give relief. The trapping season was definitely longer and easier. Open water lasted much longer in the fall and ice sometimes came and went for much of the winter. Even if snow covered the waterways, I usually had the chance that open water would appear again. I saw more clear ice for under ice 'rat and beaver trapping. The spring-holes usually stayed open all winter and were dynamite locations for most furbearers. The longer season was great for taking fur over a longer period of time. I didn't feel under the gun to catch the fur before the final freeze-up like in Minnesota. Even the dirt trapping lasted much longer, and on the wind-blown hills, dirt sets could be sometimes made all winter.

My first season in Nebraska was much about change and learning. I knew there was great potential for harvesting fur in my new home. I also learned that the local fur buyers were far from the mark when it came to fur prices. The usual thing was for them to buy the fur "in the carcass." A lot of the trappers in Nebraska knew little about skinning and handling their fur and pretty much took whatever price was offered in the round. I handled my fur and ended up selling most of it into other parts of the country. When I first came to Nebraska, most buyers were offering a dollar to a dollar-fifty for 'rats in the carcass. I was selling those same muskrats for around five dollars when I waited until the market was established. The greatest thing about the early seventies was that the fur market seemed always to be going up. Holding furs until later in the season was almost a no-brainer. I'd just trap like heck and would usually profit by holding and selling a larger lot into a seller's market. The days of returning from the fur-buyer's place somewhat dejected were in the past. Usually there were smiles and a warm feeling that all the work was really worth the effort.

After my first fall of trapping in the Cornhusker State, I returned to Minnesota for Christmas break and brought a nice load of fur to sell. I sold those furs to a buyer in Minnesota and felt I did quite well. There was little difference in the quality of the fur, from

Tracks in the Mud

those taken in Minnesota. The 'coon I caught in eastern Nebraska had beautifully colored fur. Most of them had a very silvery tone, which was much in demand. The sizes were a bit smaller, but not much. The 'rats were very comparable to southern Minnesota 'rats and of course the mink were a bit lighter brown in color. My coyotes were better than the typical rough, reddish dogs from parts of Minnesota. My buyer liked to get the Nebraska coyotes. He said it upped his average. Foxes were very comparable, and beaver were similar to southern Minnesota beaver. It's hard to get beaver as beautiful as the ones we trapped under the ice in Northern Minnesota, though. They were very dark, and the guard hairs were long and silky.

The beauty of returning to Nebraska after Christmas was that the trapping season wasn't even half over. In Minnesota the muskrat and mink season closed by the end of December, yet I could trap all fur in Nebraska until March. The weather was also pretty cooperative, and I ended up selling another lot of fur later in the new year.

My first trapping season in Nebraska ended in February. The season had gone well. The school year went well also, so I had a very enjoyable year in my new state. As spring came and traps were pulled, I looked forward to an even better season. As summer came, I made what had been the best catch of my life, when I married my wife. We were also fortunate enough to be able to find and rent a little farm house in the country. This would be a great location for my trapping activities, and it also had a nice piece of land for a big garden. We really were elated to find this new housing. Now at night we could go out and hear the coyotes yipping and yowling, oftentimes in several directions at the same time. We crossed several creeks as we drove from our house, and it was always a great joy to stop and look over the bridge railings to see the numerous racoon tracks under the bridges. Sometimes the anticipation equals the actual trapping.

Chapter 8

"The Fur Boom: A Work in Progress"

ALTHOUGH I HAD SOME YEAR-LONG DUTIES at school and also was expected to work with youth groups during the summer, we did have some free time. My wife would also be teaching the following fall and was getting some things ready for the fall term. We did, however, find lots of time to drive the countryside and explore new areas to trap. We met many of our rural neighbors and really enjoyed the visits with these folks. We often came home with eggs and produce. Most of the neighbors were also more than happy to give permission to trap on their land. My notebook began to fill up with trapping locations as well as names and descriptions of the properties. We spiraled out from our home and used maps of the county to pinpoint locations. We also marked promising spots on creeks that crossed under roads. It seems that once we looked carefully at the lay of the land, we began to see how the furbearers traveled through the various types of terrain.

In the middle of the summer, when it was very dry, I was able to gather large quantities of bone-dry dirt to be used to bed land traps when the weather froze in the winter. Many large garbage cans were stored in the shed on the property. Trapping had taught me how to think ahead and plan well before the need actually arose for various things.

Besides getting prepared for the next trapping season, we were able to freeze and can enough vegetables to feed a small army. We had enough green beans frozen to donate them to the hot lunch program at school. I think we supplied most of the green beans eaten at school for the entire school year. I was also fortunate enough to be drawn for a deer license in the lottery. Although our income was very small, we felt secure for the coming year. I think back to our grocery bills, and it seemed that if we spent five dollars a week that would have about covered it.

I was actually becoming acclimated to the plains. Here was a place which hid nothing. The prairies were honest and straight forward. They were formidable to the first settlers used to the shelter of cool forests and wooded glens, but each day on the Great Plains was bold in its direction. The winds and storms were strong and without inhibition. Here we were caught in the middle of it all. The hot, parched stubble of Kansas breathed upon us like a blast furnace in mid-summer, and the sharp tongue of Saskatchewan pierced us in the winter. The land and climate were as unpredictable and rangy as the ghostly coyotes I pursued. I would guess that when the ancestors of the present farmers and ranchers came to these plains, it was comparable to going to the moon. This was a place unlike any they had ever experienced. The people, like the rigid land that molded them, were honest and straightforward. They expected their neighbors to be as honest and reliable as the land they farmed. These were folks who would do anything to help another and the kind of folks for whom you would do the same. I recall many times when someone pulled me out of a muddy ditch and would not even hear of being compensated. They'd always say to do the same for someone else. People who live here always felt compelled to return the favor to someone. All in all it was a pretty good system.

This was a summer to learn more of the land. It was also a summer to learn more of the opportunities of a new place. The numerous reservoirs, not only were possible places to trap in the next fall, but were also great places to fish. We learned a new technique of fishing called "jug-fishing." We got a bunch of old milk jugs and wrote our name and address on them, attached a line with several hooks to each one and then baited the hooks and threw the jugs out into a lake. The jugs floated around and we hoped had fish attached to them when we pulled them in. They could be left out overnight or however long one wanted to fish. We could go back to shore and camp out and check the lines later. In Minnesota it would be considered putting out "set-lines," which are strictly illegal, but in Nebraska it was great sport. We could expect to catch almost any kind of fish, with catfish being the most sought after. It was almost like trapping for the summertime. There were no closed seasons on fish in Nebraska, and many fish had no limit on them. I also found the giant bullfrogs to be fantastic eating. These were much bigger than any frogs in my home state. The legs were almost the size of chicken legs and were really good. Of course lots of panfish and rough-fish we caught were put into the freezer for raccoon bait.

The heat of summer slipped slowly into September and school began. I had time to do a bit of hunting, and I was fortunate to fill the deer tag I had drawn, but each trip out also doubled as a scouting trip for fur. I guess I began to learn to think either high or low. The ridges, line fences, and field-roads all showed me tracks, trails, and droppings. These were the high routes frequented by the

Tracks in the Mud

land furbearers. The draws and creeks drew my attention low to the places where the water animals traveled. I began to theorize that in this country a trapper would starve on the side-hills.

The more I traveled, the more I became amazed at the numbers of racoons and coyotes in the area. Of course some places were extreme "hot-spots" and others were mediocre. I began to formulate a plan to get the best places first. I knew my time would be limited, and I wanted to be most efficient. My plan was to hit the raccoon and coyotes hard before the general water season opened. My experience was that the fur was in good condition and very sellable on these species by the first of November, and the weather was usually nice with little ice or freezing of the soil. Water sets would be easy to maintain for 'coon and the dirt sets for coyotes would need no dry dirt or anti-freeze. I had to avoid catching mink and muskrats in the racoon water sets. That was accomplished by setting footholds very deep to catch only the longer legged 'coons and avoiding the short legged mink and 'rats. All the dirt sets would have to be run before school and some of the water sets could be tended after the teaching day. There were no check laws in Nebraska at the time, but I still didn't want land-caught animals to stay in sets over the day.

As the season neared, I had mapped out where all my sets would be placed. The first day went like clockwork. Sometimes, my wife would drive the truck on the morning check, and I had only to jump out of the stopped truck and shine my light down into the water of the creeks, usually under a bridge to see if a catch had been made. The glow of raccoon eyes in the light became my queue to jump down the bank and quickly make the harvest. Sometimes I would be thrilled to see two sets of eyes in adjacent sets. I really learned the effectiveness of "gang-setting" especially in good areas. The same thing applied to the coyote trapping. Seeing the glow of two sets of coyote eyes in the headlight at either end of an earthen stock dam, as we approached was enough to get the adrenalin going on an early morning outing. There were even times when triples were taken. I can still picture three coyotes within forty feet of each other in a low crossing as I turned down a field road and shined the headlights to the location. Straining to see eyes moving in the beam of a light was one of the best parts of early morning trapping.

We still only had one vehicle at this time, so the "trapping truck" also had to get us to school. I had to get going by three in the morning if I was to get the traps checked, and then get both myself and my wife to our respective schools on time. As I look back, I realize it was a good thing we were still pretty young at the time.

The farmhouse we were renting was quite small and had no basement. There was a shed and also a small attached, unheated porch. The porch seemed the best place to skin and handle fur, and worked out pretty well until the weather got really cold. It got to the point where it was impossible to skin fur in the freezing temperatures. I finally ended up skinning in the kitchen. I still remember my wife stepping over and around beaver carcasses as I skinned beaver on the floor while she cooked supper. I guess we didn't think it was a big deal, since the fur checks from a couple months of part-time trapping were about the same as a whole year's teaching salary. Yes, fur prices were rising but teachers were terribly underpaid.

One of the best parts of these formative years in Nebraska was the fact that I was getting to know a lot of landowners. Better still, they were getting to know me. These relationships would pay nice dividends in later years. Trapping coyotes was a real plus to farmers and ranchers, and this added a lot of farms and ranches to my inventory of trapping spots. As people began to realize that I could eliminate some of the predators from their area, they even began to seek me out to trap. Besides the coyotes—which was often the species bothering landowners—there was always other fur to take. Many of the places I got permission to trap had prime creeks and also stock ponds in addition to land-setting locations for coyote. One guy who raised sheep became a particularly good friend. There were times when coyotes destroyed a lot of his stock. Not only did they kill and eat sheep, but would actually hamstring sheep and just let them lie there, bleeding to death. I took a lot of coyotes from that place, but the two large ponds and a couple of creeks probably made me more money over the years I trapped there.

Slowly, I was amassing thousands of acres of private trapping land. As the years went on, I would spend lots of time visiting each of the landowners. They were always anxious to know what I had taken on their land, and I tried to keep pretty close track so I could fill them in on the details. I keyed in on the prime stretches of the best creek-bottom areas in the counties I trapped. On some places I had exclusive permission to trap miles of these creeks. The heavy bottom areas always were the "mother-load" places for fur. The higher area in between had good crossings but the heavy concentrations of fur were in the creek areas. Beaver were also growing in abundance in Nebraska, just as in other parts of the country. When I left Minnesota, there was a ten beaver limit. In my new state there was no limit, no tagging, and very few special regulations regarding beaver trapping. They became an extra facet of trapping, sometimes being an incidental catch, but mostly they were something to do later in the season as they became more prime and other trapping slowed down.

Raccoon prices had now become very attractive. They averaged ten to twelve dollars skinned and in the grease (meaning not stretched and dried). I really did not have the time to put up 'coons and scrape the hides so they were all skinned and frozen. At the time, this was an amazing price for a furbearer as common as raccoon. I just figured every one I took was a ten-dollar bill. In the seventies a ten dollar bill was a pretty good chunk of change. A hundred 'coonskins was a small fortune to a couple of impoverished teachers.

All fur prices were advancing in the seventies. They were destined to go much higher, and in a few years the fur fever would spread in the country: rural people would fancy themselves some kind of expert trapper. Road-kill raccoons would rarely be seen along the highways, not that they weren't getting hit, but they got picked up just that fast. It was pretty easy to throw a road-kill 'coon on a fur-buyer's floor and get a check for twenty-five dollars.

Although I stalked the muddy creek bottoms by moonlight, my days were spent in the classroom. In many ways my students benefited from my trapping. As stated earlier, they were very well educated in the area of biology. I remember one day in December, the day started with a slick coating of ice on everything outside. The trees were bent over with ice, and the ground was encased in a clear armor of frozen rain. Nebraska had a habit of indecision when it came to winter weather. It wasn't a day of snow but a day of freezing rain. I had promised my science class a large mammal to dissect in class that day. What could be better than a beaver, with its large lung capacity and its unique claws? Its teeth and other special equipment for its peculiar lifestyle would teach a great deal to my students. My wife and I slipped and slid our way out to the old truck and loaded up for our day in the classroom. The back of the truck was filled with trapping paraphernalia, so of course we put all our school stuff into the front seat. Included in the school supplies was a beaver carcass wrapped up and put onto the floor. The roads were a sheet of thick ice. We made our way slowly to the main road. No gravel or salt was applied to the rural roads where we lived. As I approached the first stop sign I inched my way to the intersection. When I applied the brakes, I realized that there was no chance of stopping before the stop sign. I applied the brakes and pumped just as one should, but we didn't slow down. To my right I saw, of all things, a gravel truck coming down the road. I still remember the perception of slow motion as I entered the intersection and the gravel truck bore down on our pickup. He had no more control than I did on the ice. As he slammed into the side of our vehicle, we all just slid down the road, finally coming to a stop on the side of the road. I think the extreme ice caused the impact to be less damaging. The passenger-window was out and the side of our truck was smashed but we were fine. When the truck driver finally made his way to the passenger side of our truck and stuck his head into the window to see how we were, the first thing that greeted his eyes was a bloody beaver carcass. The initial look on his face would be hard to describe, but suffice it to say he though the worst. We finally conveyed to him that we were all right. I quickly explained to him that it was only a beaver carcass. I don't remember if I ever said what it was doing in our front seat, but he was genuinely relieved to know he hadn't killed anyone.

The rest of the day involved getting the truck officially totaled so we could find a replacement and transfer all my equipment to a new truck.

Our freezer quickly filled with furs and our trip to Minnesota for the holidays was not only to visit relatives, but also was payday for the trapper. I began to realize the value of having married a math major when we sold furs. She would have averages computed in her head before the buyer could compute the total offer. Fur buyers soon came to realize she was a formidable asset to me, the seller. These were the years when we finally began to realize what it was like to sell fur into a true seller's market. No longer would fur buyers knit pick every skin to find real or imagined flaws. They really wanted to buy fur, and they had firm markets to sell it into. We could assess the market based upon reports we read and set a goal for the average price we should receive. More buyers were showing up in the country, and the competition helped to raise prices also. We were careful to sell to reputable buyers who paid with checks that didn't bounce. That was a concern as plenty of fly-by-night operators who didn't have the financing required to operate still tried to get in on the market. Word got around about these guys plenty fast. We also began to sell some fur in Nebraska as the reputation of our fine-colored 'coon began to be known on the world market. Later we would make connections to Winnipeg, while still continuing to work with buyers connected to the European and Asian markets. More and more it proved beneficial to wait to sell. Later in the season, the prices usually peaked. Learning how to market fur paid large dividends. Getting twenty percent more for our fur was a lot easier than trapping twenty percent more fur.

I'm amazed at the incredible economy that developed in the rural areas around the fur trade. Obviously financing kept the buyers in business. I'm sure bankers loved the extra business that the fur trade created for their industry. Actual trading took place either at local fur houses or at other designated places of business. Buyers bought out of their houses, on porches, garages, basements, and other sheds. Gas stations, taverns in small towns, and bait shops became the meeting places of trappers and fur buyers. Since now there was a lot of purchasing of furbearers in the carcass, a great demand arose for people to skin and handle fur. I remember lots of high school kids who skinned for fur buyers after school. They were usually paid by the skin and some could make good money if they were fast enough.

Rates varied, but at ten cents to twenty-five cents per muskrat, kids who could skin a 'rat a minute could make good wages.

A lot of new technology developed in the fur trade. Skinning machines became fairly common. Anyone who has pulled the hide off of coyotes and raccoons knows how hard it can be to do over a long period of time. Skinning machines took the backbreaking work from that task. They were simply a winch that could be hooked to the skin that pulled the skin from the body of the coyote. Many new and specialized skinning knives came out on the market. Fleshing tools and various types of fleshing beams became available to the trapper. Many pieces of equipment formerly only available to professional fur-dressers were now being sold to trappers and fur buyers. Baits and lures proliferated, and all kinds of attractors were being sold. There were now lure-makers in almost every part of the country. It seemed to me that bringing scent and canine urine from other parts of the country would be good, putting new smells out on my trap line. Every outdoor publication had advertisements that sold trapping information or the services of people who would give trapping instructions. Good trapping instruction could definitely be a shortcut to becoming a good trapper in a short period of time.

The development and evolution of the trap itself was accelerated by the need for newer and more efficient fur-taking tools. The Montgomery Trap, a pretty good predator trap, became popular. Many new companies entered the market, some to provide cheaper traps and others to try to improve upon the designs then in use. Special baited raccoon traps were invented. Foot snares were re-invented and padded foot-hold traps came out. Countless new types of stakes, spring-loaded chains, and various devices for holding and stabilizing traps were invented. Tools for pulling stakes out of frozen soil and devices for driving stakes into frozen soil were developed. New snare-locks and new snare cable came to the forefront. Trapping sleds, trapping boats, and countless headlights and gloves were sold. Everyone had a better digging tool and a better dirt sifter for dry setting.

My second season of trapping in Nebraska went well. The diversity of fur was fun and interesting. The changing of habitats was also fascinating. I had more streams to trap than I had in Minnesota. The dry land trapping was truly better just because of the greater size of farms and ranches and the wide open country. I still had some lake and marsh type of 'rat trapping and the farm ponds were lots of fun. I missed the true marshland of Minnesota and the great fox trapping available at that time. I envied my brother, who still trapped some of our old spots, but having brought my traps to Nebraska definitely had turned out well, and I knew the potential was great. The numbers of 'coon were much beyond what I had ever experienced in Minnesota and the amount of territory available to trap was extraordinary. The competition was a bit less, although it was increasing. Yet I could see the potential for running a long-line. With a lot of work and perseverance, one could make pretty fair wages. The old childhood dream, which had been pretty much subdued by low fur prices and other realities of making a living, was beginning to re-appear. The thought of spending whole days on the trap line and even a whole season now began to fill my mind. Those precious weekend days and vacation days of getting up and staying out all day were looked forward to with great anticipation. Yet it would be a few more years before the great fur boom swept me along with it into full-time trapping.

Chapter 9
"A Blue Moon Rising"

IT SEEMS THAT THERE ARE LOTS of "good old days" over the years. For my wife and me, our first were probably those first summers spent on our little farm. School responsibilities were less intense in the summer, and our schedules were somewhat informal. We were able to spend a lot of time gardening and scouting the countryside. The warm days of summer were relaxing and seemed to fuel the desire to get back into the fall and winter months. I felt much as the furbearers must feel during the days of plenty and easy living. The summer was for me a time to experiment with new staking and stabilizing devices for traps. It was a time to build bait boxes for Conibear traps and also the time to build compartments for the truck to organize trapping equipment. Life was pretty easy and maybe even a bit easier because of the extra income from the trap line. As we began to hear the new coyote pups yipping in the evening, and the days began to shorten just a bit, we knew that the work of fall and winter was nearing again. These were indeed the growth years of the modern fur industry. We felt a very positive surge in the whole outlook of the fur business. Although the feeling was one of a very positive trend, the boom was also born out by the statistics from those years.

Owing at least in part to Minnesota's long tradition of trapping and an active fur trade, the Minnesota Department of Natural Resources has long kept records of fur harvest and raw fur prices in the state. Looking at two of the most common furbearers, the muskrat and the raccoon, I have been able to glean some interesting data from the old state fur records. I'm certain that the trends represented would hold largely true for all areas of the country.

The records show that the average number of muskrats harvested in Minnesota during the decade of the 1950s averaged around 288,000 pelts per year. During the 1960s the average increased to 383,000 muskrats per season, while during the boom-decade of the 1970s the average take per season was 488,000. Likewise the average price paid for each skin was only $.67 each during the 1950s, $.84 each during the decade of the 1960s, and then skyrocketed to an average during the roaring-seventies of $3.06 each with a peak average price of $5.90 in 1979.

The statistics for raccoon follow a similar pattern. During the 1950s about 36,500 raccoon were harvested, each season in the state both by hunting and trapping combined. During the ten years of the 1960s 48,600 raccoon pelts were harvested per season, but in the decade of the 1970s the average harvest per year was 90,300. The average price per pelt was even more telling of the amazing change in the world fur markets. During the 1950s the average price paid per raccoon was $2.55 per pelt with 1955 showing an average of only $1.00 per raccoon. The 1960s showed an average of $3.44 per skin. The amazing decade of the 1970s showed an average of $18.86 per pelt with 1978 showing the almost unbelievable average price of $45.85.

Tracks in the Mud

I suppose there's a lesson here regarding supply and demand, but we can also conclude that the potential for sustainable harvest of our fur resource is much higher than the usual harvest. Far more of our furbearers die each year of starvation, predation, and disease, than are harvested for the fur trade.

Well after the great fur boom had ended, I found myself visiting with one of the large-volume fur buyers in Minnesota. He commented that not only were the incredibly high prices a factor during the seventies, but the sheer numbers of furs sold was probably the greatest aspect of the boom. During these years he found little trouble in being able to sell 50,000 muskrats during a season, while in post-boom years of the 1990s and after 2000, it was difficult for him to find a market for 10,000 muskrats in a season.

As the fur industry grew during the formative years of the 1970s, it, of course, brought in many new trappers. Numbers of trapping licenses sold always seem to grow as the price of fur increases. I believe there were two distinct groups of trappers developing: those who had grown up in a tradition of trapping and those who were completely new to the trapping fraternity.

Some of us trapped because we truly enjoyed trapping. For us it was a way of life more than a source of income. For me it was an interesting and rewarding hobby. We enjoyed the challenge and the rewards. The sunrises and sunsets gave us the promise of a new day of excitement and intrigue and the promise of a new fullness that would be revealed the following day. Of course as the money became more attractive, people were drawn to trapping merely for the money. Less-experienced trappers meant more mistakes were made out in the field. People placed sets where they didn't belong. Trespassing onto private property by people who didn't obtain permission from landowners became more common. Soon trappers had a public relations battle to fight. Those who were ethical and conscientious about the trapping trade needed to convince people of the validity of trapping to an increasingly hostile public. We knew that trapping is a valid and very selective method of harvesting a renewable resource, but we began to get some bad press, based upon the mistakes of novice and in some cases greedy trappers.

Until this time, trapping had been regarded as a very noble and reputable occupation. Trappers were never associated with money or unethical behavior. Now the press had a field day with a few cases of misjudgment. So-called animal rights groups used the hard-working trapping community as a scapegoat and as a vehicle to raise large sums of money for their bogus causes. A few doctored photos were spread into advertisements and films and soon the solid conservation-minded trapping community was portrayed as a bunch of blood-thirsty tyrants. Almost all the trappers I know are people who love the land and the wild creatures that inhabit that land. They intimately know and appreciate the wildlife, which they selectively harvest in a renewable manner. Trappers are the ones who lobby for habitat improvement and put their money where their mouths are by donating to projects that will sustain and enhance wild areas. These are the real outdoorsmen, who really know the ways of the natural world and more than any others want to keep it preserved. It always seems that if a commodity has monetary value, it will be preserved and protected, and so it is with our fur resources. Once it is relegated to only something to look at, few will really care about that resource any more.

I felt myself entering a new era of trapping. I had always taken trapping as a right I could enjoy as long as I played by the rules. Now I realized there were those who would try to impose their values upon me and in so doing take the rights I had taken for granted away from me. The good news was that trappers were beginning to organize and become proactive. I joined the Nebraska Fur Harvesters and immediately realized the benefits. The group became interested in education, to help new trappers become better, more selective, and more humane. Meetings emphasized education and drew upon experienced trappers to help train new recruits. Meetings also brought together people who sold new equipment and taught trappers to use it. We attended our first fall meeting of the Fur Harvesters and met many people who followed the trap line. We learned a lot and bought some new supplies. I met some of the best trappers in the business at the time. I learned that even the best in the business all achieved success by hard work and smart operation. There were no magic tricks to big fur catches. Good methods and good territory, coupled with hard work and long hours paid off with a nice fur check.

    I found that trappers were a bunch who shared ideas and learned from each other. All in all, trappers were a tough bunch to organize, but they were a group with such a heartfelt kinship they organized in a most natural way. I don't ever remember another parking lot packed with ninety-five percent pickup trucks, but it was a very awe-inspiring sight. I had arrived home. The essence of the heartland was in that place, the epitome of flyover country was here and in my mind it was the best place on earth. People camped and visited and swapped trapping stories. Books could have been written from the talk on the grounds of the rendezvous. We returned home with new ideas, new inspiration, and a feeling that we were not alone in our beliefs of right and wrong. We knew we shared the same dream of freedom and the love of wide-open spaces.

    You definitely come away from a trappers' convention knowing that you are not a member of a cookie-cutter bunch. Although everyone there wanted to enjoy the outdoors by pursuing furbearers, there weren't any two who did it the same way. There were a lot of good ideas, all of them different. Despite the great independence and individuality among trappers, it seemed that everyone agreed we must be proactive and aggressive in educating the public about our trade. We were beginning to be assaulted by animal rights groups and the media. Trapping organizations sprang up in every state and the lure of education and new ideas really enticed trappers to join these groups. Higher fur prices not only brought more trappers into the arena, but also gave greater desire to preserve the heritage and keep trapping regulations sensible, allowing a profitable and renewable harvest of our fur resources.

Trapper groups now began to focus in areas that were causing bad public relations for trappers. States began to outlaw anything but smooth-jawed traps. The concept of toothed traps was really obsolete anyway and they were seldom used. They were, however, endlessly shown in the anti-trapping advertisements to an uneducated and unknowing public. Twenty-four-hour check laws were put into effect, thus assuring the shortest time for trapped animals to be retained. Immediate killing sets were stressed. Some states began to mandate the completion of trapper-education courses for new trappers. New recruits to the trap line learned to make effective and humane sets. They were able to bypass the long trial-and-error process that was the only education many of us could get when it came to trapping. State Natural Resource Departments were very cooperative with trapper groups and really supported them. Local wildlife departments stood behind the trappers as an effective and intelligent tool of resource management and as harvesters of a renewable product. Trappers themselves, volunteered many hours in education and also helped in coordination with local game enforcement personnel.

Effective and safe use of killer-type traps was taught and this relatively new and very humane tool came into the forefront. I had the experience of a large Conibear trap springing on my arm. The simple precaution of having a piece of rope in my pocket I could use to release the springs and, therefore, free myself from the trap, saved me from wearing the trap back to the truck or even worse, wearing it all the way home.

Getting to know other trappers was a great experience. Of course I knew many friends and relatives who trapped when I grew up, but getting to meet trappers who grew up with different traditions was very interesting. I guess the type of terrain and the species of furbearers in a particular trapper's area had much to do with the traditions that influence that trapper. I grew up in Minnesota and learned to trap on waterways for muskrats and mink. Here I met folks who grew up on the prairies of the West and cut their teeth on coyotes. Some of these guys had slid up and down the slimy banks of muddy streams all their lives pursuing mostly 'coon. I was really learning to broaden my horizons. A lot of experiences came together at trappers' get-togethers. Although most trappers enjoyed the solitude of being in the outdoors alone, the human side of trapping also became an important aspect of the endeavor. After all, we do produce a product worn by people. If we don't understand the human side of our profession. we miss a large part of the whole picture.

A number of publications also came out that were specifically for trappers. Of course the old Harding Magazine *Fur-Fish-Game* had always been a magazine trappers could go to for trapping information and even fur market prognostications. Now *The Trapper* magazine came out, which was almost exclusively a trappers' publication. There were many "how-to" articles and also good market information. The advertising was also great in that it showed the new products out there for trappers. A few trapping articles found their way into some of the other outdoor magazines that usually were primarily hunting and fishing magazines.

Another thing I learned to do during these years prior to going full time at trapping, was to run trapping as a business. I began to log mileage and keep receipts for supplies. As alluded-to earlier, log books and maps became common pieces of equipment in the truck. I found that specialized types of protective clothing could also be deducted as expenses. The reality of taxation became the mother of invention as I learned to deduct all my costs of production. There were also rumblings of gas rationing during these years of the first great oil crisis. It was thought that any legitimate business might not be subject to such rationing. My little fur company became an entity and a legitimate business. Soon I would also enlist the services of an accountant to make sure all my documentation was correct. Although I enjoyed what I did, it was comforting to find that trapping was actually turning a profit. These were wonderful lessons that carried over into other business ventures later in my life.

The secret was now out of the bag when it came to trapping methods. No longer were old long-liners carefully guarding their special sets and mysterious methods. Many of the big-name trappers were offering personal instructions. Instruction became the off-season job for many trappers. In fact I actually wonder if trapping lessons may have been the principal source of income for many trappers. Indeed the supply, instructions, and lure-making businesses thrived. I remember talking to some local folks in Broadus, Montana, who said the local post office had to expand its facilities when Craig O'Gorman brought his lure-making business to that small southeastern Montana town.

I don't doubt that a lot of these professional trappers could put up good numbers of fur, but rumor had it that some of them did some fancy photos at the fur buyers place to promote their lures and instructions. There were photos of a pickup load of beaver, which was supposed to be a day's catch, or a barn with its side covered with coyote pelts and then an offer for complete instruction in the dynamite methods which took such phenomenal catches. Again the major thing that seemed to lead to large catches was good fur territory, hard work, long hours, and efficient operation. Some of the trapping instructions did stress trap line layout and methods of rotation and just plain smooth, well-organized operation. Some of the books also had good tips on these topics as well. I still believe that some of the best trappers were those who never published any methods or gave any instruction. They just got out and produced the fur and took home good honest fur checks.

    As I look back at those days of the early seventies I know that at the time it didn't seem like anything historical was afoot. Prices on fur were rising and numbers of trappers were increasing, but the land looked the same and if any one would have said that there was a new wind blowing in the fur trade I would have probably not given it a second thought. Only once in a blue moon could all the forces come together to produce such times for the trapper. To me it was fun, a supplement to our income, and a wonderful diversion to one who was confined to a classroom all day. I still had it pretty much stuck in my mind that trapping was only a hobby.

Chapter 10
"Part-Time Bliss- Riding the Learning Curve"

*I*T WAS PROBABLY THE SECOND WINTER after we got married, the seventy-four and seventy-five trapping season, that we took a bunch of green-skinned racoons to a local fur buyer. We probably needed some money and felt it would be good to sell the early caught skins since we had heard prices were pretty good. We dumped fifty or sixty skins on the floor, and the buyer counted them up at a straight twelve dollars each without even looking at them. He didn't even try to throw out the smaller ones. We were thrilled but of course we sold a lot of raccoon later that season at even higher prices. The market really was beginning to rise during those years. I still had the mentality that 'coon usually sold for three to five dollars. Twelve seemed incredible. Also, at that time it was a lot of money, the dollar being worth a lot more than now. Gas was still well under a dollar a gallon, raccoon were plentiful, and it really didn't take too much to produce them. Those were the years when coyotes also really spiked in price. They were following a red fox market, which was getting into the thirty-to-forty-dollar range. I had never known long-haired furs to be worth that much money until the seventies. Of course I had grown up in the sixties, when only 'rats and mink really had any value at all.

It was really a great phenomenon to have the fur market continue to trend upward for so many years. Great confidence rose in the price of fur, and people were ready to invest in traps and equipment. Fur buyers were making money, and I suppose they were able to get financing and felt confident in investing in fur. It became a pretty healthy industry. In addition to the great demand for our wild fur, fur ranchers were also doing well. I suppose as they proliferated their herds, and more people got into the fur farming business, the old supply-and-demand thing caught up with us. The seventies though, were very bullish on fur. It was truly an exciting time to be involved with the fur trade.

Again, this trapping season meant long hours and hard work for a teacher-trapper. Mornings were still early, but now we had traps that could be checked on the way to school. That meant we headed out early enough so that I could check traps and then change clothes at school before classes began. The evenings found us doing the same thing in reverse. I remember many times my wife would be correcting papers in the cab of the truck while I was checking traps. Bless her heart, sometimes she would be correcting my papers as well. It was great to have her as a driver also. When I had a section of creek where I had permission on a whole mile, she would drop me off on one road, and while I checked traps through the section, she would drive around to the other side of the section and pick me up. This saved a lot of back-tracking. Sometimes we would drive to the middle of a section on a field road, and I would check traps out to the road and she would pick me up at that point. I remember driving up to trapped coyotes on various farms. While I re-made the sets, she would be judiciously correcting papers for the next day's classes. We proceeded through the season with only one vehicle and operated very efficiently. Later in the evening, to the sound of pelts being peeled from muskrats and racoons, my wife completed lesson plans for the next day. I wondered how many part-time trappers did the same things. Even now the similar scenario is repeated by those dyed-in-the-wool harvesters of wild fur.

After Christmas, the routine slowed some, but there were always the coyote sets and snares as well as the under-ice beaver sets to tend. The big attraction was always the spring holes in the streams, which seemed to be fur-magnets all winter. Mink, muskrats, and some very nice winter-prime raccoons were always interested in checking out the open water in those areas. As the fur began to show signs of rubbing and becoming over-prime, sets were pulled. Some of the badgers I took during those late winter thaws were the most beautiful furs I remember. Sometimes during the early coyote season in late October and early November, badger would be taken, and they were obviously of "paintbrush" quality with little under-fur. Since I knew they were of little value, I usually tried to release them. Believe me, they were not an easy critter to release. They usually had the trap-site so dug up that it looked like an open pit iron mine. Getting the spring release poles onto the trap springs was a challenge, but sometime these same animals would be caught later in the season and the change in the fur was unbelievable. These prime badgers had fur that was four inches long and the color in Nebraska was a beautiful platinum blond. One fur buyer who bought them from me in Minnesota said that he never got prime badgers in Minnesota because most of them were caught in early fall in fox sets and by the time the fur was prime in Minnesota, the badgers were long into hibernation. In Nebraska, they stayed out later and came out during

Tracks in the Mud

the frequent thaws. Prime badger were one of the perks of late-season trapping.

As the trapping slacked off, I did get to do some ice fishing on the numerous reservoirs. The variability of the winters in Nebraska can best be explained by referencing the ice-fishing. There were some winters that put close to three feet of ice on those lakes, and there were others when it was hard to find enough ice to get out fishing. Some winters saw low temperatures only in the teens above zero. Other winters recorded temperatures well below zero. Sixties in mid-winter were not unheard of, but when it happened you had better brace yourself for temperatures fifty or sixty degrees colder within a few hours. I really learned to play the weather when trapping. Thaws needed to be taken advantage of, and fronts were the times to have lots of sets out. Many large buck mink were dug out of the snow after a blizzard roared through.

After this season, we realized that a second vehicle would be very helpful. We both had busy schedules, and my wife began to have after school commitments. A second car would give us both more flexibility, especially during trapping season. The other thing we began to realize was that we would love to have our own home. We knew we wanted to get a place out in the country. We began the search, and finally found the perfect place. It was near my trapping areas but also gave closer access to some new areas. It was a bit of a fixer-upper but certainly a very livable house. It had a full basement for skinning and handling fur and also a double garage. We were able to make it a reality, and the idea of our own place was very exciting. We made the move with not too many pickup-loads of stuff. It was nice to have a pretty decent garage to store my trapping equipment and also a basement where I could set up an efficient place to skin and stretch fur. A fleshing beam and permanent skinning gambrel were a luxury I had not had before. No more would my wife have to step over me as she made supper and I skinned fur. There was also plenty of space for freezers and also room to hang furs and stretchers. I could boil and wax traps in the back yard and have plenty of room to hang them up until the season.

At this time I was also beginning another seasonal business oriented to the summer months. It also fit in pretty well with teaching. It seems that all the teachers I knew at the time were moonlighters, who needed other sources of income. My summer occupation would lend itself well to my later foray into full-time trapping. Now that I look back, maybe teaching was a natural lead-in to professional trapping. I was no stranger to long hours and mediocre pay. In either occupation I worked day and night and the pay stayed the same. Education was also important in both occupations. When teaching, I tried to impart an education. When trapping I seemed to get an education. If anyone thinks he can avoid having to learn new things when trapping he would be badly mistaken. I felt like during these last couple of years, I was getting my master's degree in the fur business. Not only did I have to continue to learn new methods of actual harvest of the fur, but marketing and general business procedures were also important. I knew that just like I did my student-teaching and practical training in college, I was getting my education not only from the animals I pursued but also from the fur buyers, the tax accountants, and the various authors who wrote books on trap-line efficiency.

If there is any animal capable of giving one an education, it's the coyote. My next season really brought that concept home. My first couple of years of trapping coyotes was spent on relatively uneducated animals. There was a large population and lots of pups, which were easy to catch. They were just like big fox, as earlier mentioned. Once I got the equipment sized properly, they seemed easy to take. Now the competition became a factor. Coyotes were encountering sets more frequently. Due to mistakes by others as well as by me, more coyotes had been harassed and wizened to various sets. Now I began to see tracks approach sets and yet the coyote didn't work the set at all. I began to mix up the lures and types of sets. More post sets, which replicated a place where a coyote had marked his territory, were used. The old "flat set" taught to me by a trapper from out in the Sand Hills also began to work better than the usual dirt-hole set. Some animals actually became shy of anything associated with bait, lure, and even in some cases something as natural as coyote urine at the set location. More and more I learned that some coyotes had to be taken with trail sets and snares. I just had to learn even more intricately what their habits were. I also learned that the early time was the time to kill the numbers, before many of the youngsters got educated.

Even the raccoon taught me a lot about proper trap placement. It's not hard to get a lot of sprung traps when trapping raccoon. I had adopted the practice of using a lot of good strong single number one long-spring traps for 'coon. Many sources recommend at least number one-and-a-half traps for this species. I found they could be held easily on the slippery mud banks of these streams, if staked properly and caught across the toes. The only draw-back for the smaller traps was that placement had to be exactly correct or sprung traps would be frequent. My reasoning was that I could afford a lot more traps by using the smaller sizes and, therefore, more sets could be made. I, of course, found trapping to be a numbers game. The more sets, the more fur caught. The smaller traps were quick and easy to set and could be carried easily to the locations. Just like any other occupation, the more one did it, the better one become at it. So with trapping, I think I improved at it with each set made.

If larger catches make more money, selling correctly also increased the value of the catch. Some good fur buyers taught me a lot about grading fur. Now I knew exactly what I had before I went to market. In fact I knew as I removed an animal from a set what it was worth. At the end of the day, I could calculate what the day's fur should bring and profitability could be determined immediately as I figured expenses. I also learned a lot about handling fur. I began to flesh and stretch all my 'rats and, of course, stretched all my coyotes and fox. I also learned that, for me, it wasn't worth the time needed to scrape and dry raccoon. They were all skinned and frozen. I could skin a muskrat a minute and could go through a pile of raccoon in a short amount of time. I learned to skin with hip boots on and really dig in and get it done. I hated to spend all my time at home in the basement with the furs.

During these years, I also learned to avoid like the plague those fur buyers who graded furs into lots of piles. They usually paid a very high price for a small portion of the lot but then graded down to very low prices on some. I found that a straight average was almost always the best. I always went with an average per pelt in mind and if a buyer didn't meet that without a very good reason I didn't sell. I kept daily tabs on the market. I talked to trappers, read the reports, and talked to buyers. Always took with a grain of salt, what trappers say they got for their fur. They tended to talk about the highest price for a pelt. Ask the average with all the pelts included, even the low-grades, and one could get a real idea of what was paid. Some buyers definitely can do better on certain items, depending on what kind of market they had. Marketing became more fun as I really learned to know fur and its many grades. Of course selling into an advancing market was also a big plus.

Record keeping also became a much bigger thing for me. Notebooks logged set locations and numbers. Records of catches at various locations helped me know how the harvest was going in various places. Maps became indispensable. Accurate record keeping for the accountant also became more and more precise. My schooling was reaching a new level.

The fall of 1976 found both my wife and I teaching full time at the same school. This was really great. We could travel to school together and our schedules coordinated pretty well. That fall also found us entering a new era in our personal lives as we were expecting our first child. I think that the specter of that extra responsibility of a child brings out the "squirrel instinct" in both parents. We expanded our garden and froze and canned enough vegetables to feed half the county. Perhaps the killer instinct also was heightened in me. The search for new trapping territory was relentless. In our new area, I began to meet all the neighboring farmers. Most were quite agreeable to have me trap their land.

As I stepped outside on those fall nights and the train hit the crossing at the little town to the northeast of us with a blast from its whistle, I would hear the "song dogs" light up in several directions from our house. The hair on the back of my neck stood up as I thought of the fine locations I had obtained permission to trap. In each direction from our house were prime areas where the line fences met, and the field roads intersected with tree lines. Every place where the tracks and droppings hit the roads was etched in my mind, and I visualized the families of coyotes as they crossed their areas in the constant hunt for food. I guessed I would hunt for food in these areas as well, making the hunters the hunted. My senses seemed heightened now as I too felt the need to provide for a growing family. One feels that primal instinct for family survival as one becomes a parent. To some it meant longer hours at the office or overtime on the construction site. To me it began to mean more hours searching the hills and creek bottoms for such telltale signs as a hair caught on a barbed wire fence or the scratch marks at a special rise in the terrain. The places where I could meet the quarry face to face stood out in my imagination, and I visualized the gray forms in the early morning light, tied to their inconspicuous spots on the land.

Chapter 11

"A New Baby and Old Dreams"

MY WIFE AND I FOUND OURSELVES on that late October Saturday, involved in the squirrel-like preparations for the coming winter. I planned to get a pickup load of manure for the garden from a neighbor and also wanted to do some last minute scouting of various trapping areas. My wife decided to ride along. It was approaching late October, and our baby was due very soon. There were a few times as we bumped along on dirt roads and crossed railroad tracks that she seemed a bit uncomfortable. We figured it went with the territory of being close to a delivery date. I still remember the abundant fur sign as we traveled the countryside on that Saturday. It hadn't rained for a while and the coyote tracks in the dusty field roads got me pretty excited. I was at the point where I had literally hundreds of set locations already planned. I had formulated how the areas would be set, in what sequence the farms would be trapped, and how many coyotes, 'coons, and other furbearers I should catch in each area. I knew that much of my early coyote trapping would be done within close proximity to our house. I wanted to be able to check coyote sets before school.

We enjoyed that October day, talking about the land, the various neighbors we had met, and of course the arrival of our child. I suppose names came up, as well as the need to have everything ready for the arrival of our little one. We knew we would be very busy with teaching, taking care of the new arrival, and of course the arrival of the trapping season and its demands. We were fortunate to have good arrangements for child care so that my wife could resume teaching after the birth. This turned out to be our last, long, lazy, fall day to enjoy, for the next day our first daughter arrived. It was a Sunday to remember. We had planned to go to church and spend the afternoon with various projects that teachers only get to complete on weekends. I had thought about maybe putting in a couple of leisurely coyote sets on a neighbor's place, just to check the fur for primeness and to help calm the trapping fever that was now raging within.

More pressing matters appeared, and I was amazed at how quickly the blessed event took place. We found ourselves rushing to town and the hospital where we were pre-registered. I rushed to get the gown on that allowed me to be in the delivery room. Our little six-and-a-half pound "keeper" arrived very quickly. All went well, and the stay at the hospital was short. Not only did our school give my wife some time off, they also granted me a week of paternity leave. This was almost an unheard of concept in 1976, but I gladly accepted the time off.

My mother-in-law came to our place to help with the baby, and I was not needed around the house a great deal. You guessed it right! The coyote trapping season was about to begin in earnest. Seldom had I had a block of time such as this to trap coyotes.

I decided to operate within about a ten-mile radius of our house. I could check back periodically to see if I was needed for anything, yet I would be able to run a pretty full-time trap line for the week. Of course by this time all the equipment was ready, the locations for sets were planned, and it took very little time to be pounding steel in earnest. The weather had been cool that fall, and even a bit of snow was in the air the day our daughter was born. I was confident the fur was pretty good, so I was ready to really "go for it."

It turned out to be a beautiful week, and the catch was great. I wasn't sure just what my mother-in-law was thinking as I carried all those dead yodel-pups into the basement and removed their skins, but when we told her what we hoped they'd be worth, she cheered me on. Long story short, on the financial end of it, any hospital bills that weren't covered by insurance would be paid for in coyote fur.

I think this week was pivotal for me as a trapper. I realized what I could accomplish on a full-time trap line. I saw the pieces fall into place and really pay off in a fast, efficient catch. All the pre-planning, scouting, and preparations made it a profitable and enjoyable week. The most exciting part of the week was the sense each day that I could keep going, even after the sun came up. The feel of doing this full time during the week when most folks were at some other job was like a new horizon being reached. I actually had a minute or two to see the sun rise, watch the specter of white clouds of coyote breath rising in a sparkling clear morning and seeing the frost that clung to the fur on that coyote's neck where he was held for my arrival. These were moments that I felt I could repeat many times over and never get tired of. The shear joy of strapping on a pack basket and walking into a set location and the feeling of returning to the truck with a heavy varmint slung over my shoulder was overpowering. I could visualize myself in another time, another era, and feel a bond with all trappers from times past to the present. I guessed that the mountain men of a hundred years ago felt the cold air in their nostrils and heard the same sounds of a day beginning and looked upon the world much as I did on those fall days.

My week's foray into full-time wolfing came quickly to an end, however, and the duties of teaching and parenthood mandated a part-time trapping schedule for the rest of the season. Yet the memory of those days stirred the old dream in my heart, the dream that began when I was a kid wearing one black hip boot and one green one. These were the two that leaked the least from a couple of old discarded pairs. It was the dream that kept me sane as I attended school and waited out the bookish hours until I could get back outside. It was the same dream I had told myself was a dream of the past, one that could never be realized in these modern times. I had convinced myself I was born too late for that dream and put it out of my mind. Now again, I wondered as the shreds of that dream danced in my mind.

The world actually settled down a bit after the birth of our little girl. To be sure, nights were interrupted, and some of the most tired days of our lives were upon us. Yet, the world didn't end, our lives still were filled with lots of new and wonderful things, and the trap line still was a big part of my enjoyment. To be sure things were changing. Gas prices were at sixty cents a gallon, nearly twice what they had been in 1972, yet they weren't rationing gas and the feeling was that at least we could get enough. The price was very high compared to what we had grown up with, but the scare of the Oil Embargo was past, and I felt that from a trapping standpoint, money could be made with the fur prices also rising.

Those early-caught coyotes turned out to be very much worth the effort. When we later sold my coyotes in one lot from the whole season, they all went at a straight average which was about forty or forty-five dollars. The long-hair market was continuing to move upward. Our daughter chose an extremely good time to be born. It was the perfect week to have paternity leave, and the perfect lead-in to the water trapping season.

Tracks in the Mud

The concentration of coyotes made them pretty profitable. I didn't have to cover a lot of area, especially early in the season when the family groups were still pretty much intact. Double catches at locations were fairly frequent, and that really upped the average per trip.

The place where we lived before we bought our house was west of our present home. I had established a lot of trapping territory in that area and would trap it later when I could pursue all the fur after the water season opened. This would make it more efficient. Now I had begun to work east and had developed a trap line to the direction of our residence. I was developing two distinct areas, one to the west and one to the east. The terrains differed a bit, and there arose a bit of diversity in my two areas. On a part-time basis, I had to work the areas separately, there being not enough time to set out in two directions each day. Later the two distinct areas would offer some great full-time possibilities.

I was going through the dilemma of specialization. Land trapping and water trapping were quite different, and the equipment, traps, baits, and preparation are different in each endeavor. Keeping traps clean and bait separate from traps was very important when dry-land trapping for coyotes. Clean traps meant less dug-out traps. Coyotes were supposed to concentrate on the hole or attractor and not smell the trap buried there to catch them. Cleanliness was next to Godliness when trapping coyotes. Water trapping on the other hand was a very muddy, dirty, all-out smelly-bait business, especially when trapping 'coon. My experience during this season with specifically trapping only coyotes for a week proved the potential of this type of specialization. Yet as I drove farther from home, it began to make sense to take all the available fur on my route. Land trapping with hip boots on was certainly fine, even preferable when kneeling at trap-sites all day, but the separation of equipment demanded special care. Over the years, I worked out a system with some specialization at certain times, which also allowed me to take all fur-types at other times. Having a fur market with all furs valuable wasn't a bad problem to have, but it was funny how these seemingly insignificant changes in procedure can make so much difference in the success of a trapping season.

I was now in my fifth year of teaching. Being a teacher was really teaching me a lot. I came to enjoy the students a great deal. They were truly the brightest aspect of being a teacher. They never seemed to tire of knowing more, and I learned that the joy of being a kid was lost on some adults. I had the great luck of working with some wonderful and dedicated staff members. My teaching experience was a great one so far. Yet, I began to look down the road to the future and wondered if I could picture myself as a teacher or school administrator thirty years down the path of life.

Each day I was captured by the enthusiasm of my students, and I was entranced by the sunshine or clouds, or even by the snow that swirled past my classroom windows. I looked forward more and more to the time spent outside.

At the time we were developing another summertime business that held potential for income and also would allow for fall and winter months available for other pursuits. My wife was and still is totally in love with teaching. I could see that people like her should be in the classroom. But I was beginning to wonder if it was what I should continue doing. The thought of having fall and winter months available to trap full time was more than appealing. I began to visualize the intersection of a robust fur market, a great trapping territory, and myself with full-time availability to trap.

We had to crunch the financial numbers and it had to work out. With my wife's salary plus her great health insurance plan plus my summer income, I could see how much income the trap line needed to provide, for us to survive financially. My decision was based upon solid information as well as my great desire to fulfill a dream. My principal told me that more people felt badly about things they didn't do, than things they did. Of course the immortal wisdom of Yogi Bera rang true as well: "When you come to a fork in the road, you better take it."

What would cause one to become a full-time trapper? That's a question that if asked when I was younger would have been answered with: "If I can, then I would." I suppose the bottom line now was that I could be a full-time trapper. As we looked at finances, fur prices, potential trapping territory, and equipment, it looked to us that I could. The greatest thing for me was to have a wife who always supported me. She wanted me to be happy and to be all that I could be. Bless her heart, as she told me if that's what I wanted to do I should do it. She has never been one to worry about things and she had total faith that this would be a good thing. She never has been a worrier and she never had a doubt that we would be just fine financially if I stopped teaching. As things turned out, it was a good decision.

If I had known I was living in the greatest fur boom in history and I was in a position to be a full-time trapper in that fur boom, I would have been elated. I guess that living in a great boom of some economic significance was much like living in a recession. One doesn't really know its happening until it's over. I was about to be a full-time player, a practicing participant in an historic event, albeit an event that most people really didn't know was happening. We who harvested fur during the seventies were a kind of underground movement. We went about our profession in a mode of stealth and quiet determination. We ran against the grain of all political correctness. We operated as historical throw-backs, lost in a time of modernization, yet caught up in an ancient and intricate mode of individual freedom. We were caught in the high point of the rise and fall of a big cycle.

The thought of being able to run a full-time trap line was of course very appealing. I knew that to do the best possible job at it, the season had to be planned, yet flexibility is always important as weather and fur numbers can and do change. Fur prices were also a large factor. I would want to be on top of the highest priced fur, but numbers and ease and efficiency of harvest also were important. The highest priced fur maybe wouldn't be the most profitable.

Chapter 12

"New Days, Old Ways, In the Golden Haze"

NOW THAT THE DECISION had been made to trap full time, preparation must begin. The first thing I did was to get the latest trapping regulations. Each season the laws seemed to change as the Game and Parks Commission attempted to manage the fur resource. My first year at full-time trapping would see laws with little change from the previous season. The 'coon season would open on November first, and the general water season would commence on November fifteenth. To me, that meant about ten days of specialized coyote trapping until the 'coon season opened. I wanted to hit the coyotes hard on all of my permission areas when they were still grouped up and in the families before the dispersion. When trapping only coyotes where I could drive to all sets through the gated field roads, much area could be covered and I could run both east and west each day. I still wanted to be able to check all land sets in one day. We did have a two-day check law, which would work well for me when water trapping. The day before the first of November, the coyote traps would be pulled, and I would hit the bridge trapping very hard for two weeks. The idea was to take as many raccoon as possible from the public right of ways along the roadways in the two weeks before the mink and muskrat season opened.

The exclusive 'coon line would be extended to a two-day line, one day running east in a big loop and the other day running west in a loop. The water sets would allow for dead 'coon in properly made water sets. With multiple sets at each location I could catch two night's worth of fur and pick it up with one check. The efficiency of the two-day line and the great amount of territory covered made sense to me.

The laws really did the final molding and framing of the trap line. They determine the equipment and the sequence of the operation. Other laws that were important to me were those that determine the types of traps that are legal. The 220 Conibear was legal for most set locations and it surely was a great asset to 'coon production. The 330 Conibear was only allowed as a submerged water set, making it primarily a beaver tool. Multiple-catch cage traps were allowed for muskrat trapping, and I built a good number of them for use in those particularly good muskrat runs. The date and openings as discussed earlier of course determined the whole framework of the season for me. Now as a full-time trapper, the midweek openings were an advantage, since it gave me the jump on the part-time weekend trappers. The length of the seasons allowed me to split my season and hit the public areas hard early and save my private lands for later in the season.

Another thing that was important was the application required to get special permits to trap state lakes and reservoirs. By submitting an application to the Game and Parks Commission you were put into their lottery and assigned one or more lakes to trap. Some of these were really good. The productiveness hinged upon yearly fur numbers and water levels. If I drew a good lake, it could be left until a bit later in the season while I trapped the public lakes first.

Not only were the trapping regulations important, but the laws that regulate other users of the outdoors also affected my trapping activity. The dates of the pheasant season were important to me. I knew that if I trapped coyotes heavily before the November opener of the bird-hunting season, I would have no problems with hunting dogs tampering with my coyote sets. When the pheasant season opened I would be working the water sets which would be little affected by hunters' dogs. Later when the major bird hunting was done, I would again trap coyotes. I would work the lakeshore sets during the week when the waterfowl hunters were probably at work, and thus avoid confrontations with duck-hunters. The plan was to do my work on the trap line with little impact on other outdoor activity. The bottom line would be less harassment of my operation and less chance of stolen fur or traps.

We were now entering into record territory when it came to fur value. Most people knew the value of fur. Most trappers were honest and minded their own business, but there were always folks out there who would steal fur from traps and also take traps. It pretty much went with the territory, and I finally began to just write it off as a cost of doing business. I had never been able to get over the frustration of that sort of thing and it really angered me. It was no different than if someone came into my home and walked off with my TV or the rifle mounted on the wall.

Hiding sets and concealing the catch after it was made became very important to my operation. There was of course great joy in trapping on the private land which I spent many days procuring. Once the hectic days of trapping the cream from the public areas was over, the season of harvesting fur from private lands was most enjoyable.

One thing that changed for me was the motivation for the way I ran my trap line. I had always considered trapping a form of recreation. Now I needed to consider profitability first as I operated my trap line. Certainly trapping was still an enjoyable activity, yet I now felt the need to run trapping as a business.

The preparation for that first full-time run at trapping began early in the summer before the season opened. Equipment was readied early, and trips to trapping areas and visits with landowners took place at a leisurely pace during the whole summer and fall. I found it much easier to find farmers at home with time to talk during the summer than when they were busy with either harvest or planting.

I purchased about one hundred more traps of various types. I built bait boxes for 220 Conibears. Many stakes were made. There would be no improvising any kind of stake or drag on location. All fastening devices would be in the truck and ready to be used. I found a pile of old oak flooring and realized that great 'coon stakes could be made from the narrow, but strong, pieces of oak. When these were pushed into the hard mud bottom of the streams, no way could any raccoon pull them out. I still had many of these stakes twenty years later or more. They cost me nothing and stood the test of time. I also made many steel stakes for dry land sets, and some were also used in water drowning sets. All my 110 Conibears were staked and ready. Bait was prepared and put into containers and either frozen or preserved in jars. Every bit of preparation short of setting the traps in the locations was done. Locations were marked on maps and written down in notebooks. Dry dirt was gathered and put into large garbage cans, ready for the later frozen ground trapping. I built stabilizer stakes for trail-set Conibears and snares. More stretchers were built or bought to accommodate the

Tracks in the Mud

fur I hoped to catch. An extra freezer was bought to freeze skinned hides. Last but not least, new tires were put on to the truck and it was checked out thoroughly.

I now organized the traps into various types and put them into wooden boxes so I could load them by the box and know exactly how many traps were in each box. Stakes were bundled into groups of the same number to coincide with the numbers of traps in a box. Digging tools and rubber gloves were organized, and lure bottles were put into boxes and organized so I could find the various types of lures. There were bait lures, call lures for pulling the fur in from long distances, and lures made from various parts of the predators. Coyote and fox urine were purchased by the gallon. Of course fishing was a part of the job as well, because fish were the primary bait for racoon trapping. Sometimes I believe these summer activities were as much fun as the actual trapping in the fall and winter. The anticipation often was much better than the realty that came later.

When one planned so much, the actual opening day can be anticlimactic. I'd pictured and visualized the actual setting of the traps so much that it seemed almost like I had been there before, even when it was the first day of the season. Yet, having a precise game plan was worth its weight in gold. There were always things that came up that could alter the precise implementation of the plan but following the game plan for the most part does pay dividends.

As the season approached I had time to think about how the land was woven together with trails of furbearers and their intersection with my activity. The hills were pearled between the liquid ribbons of the streams and punctuated with the numerous stock dams. What a blessing to tie oneself to the land and fly upon the wings of a season of hope. It was a blank palette, this idea of trapping full time. There was an open-endedness about it that breathed an eternal freedom into my soul. Each day had only the limitation of twenty-four hours. There would be no other rules.

One day of that fall stands out for me. It was a day around or shortly after Labor Day. I still remember the wet dew on the grass and the bright sun coming up. One of those fallish days in Nebraska, it started out a bit like autumn but ended up much like a summer day. I was outside early, working on preparations for the trapping season or possibly working on some aspect of another business. My wife came out the door with our daughter and was all dressed up for school. It was the first day of the school year, and she was about to leave for her teaching job. For the past twenty-one years of my life I had headed off to school on that day. Today I would be left behind and at the same time I was leaving behind a way of life to which I had grown accustomed. I would miss the ride to school during which we had talked and prepared ourselves for the day. I visualized my students coming to class and meeting a new teacher. I hoped, as all teachers must, that my former students would talk about how I had done things the year before. Soon though, they would grow accustomed to a new teacher, and I would continue to miss the buzz of the classroom, even as I went on to do new and exciting things. People leave a little part of themselves in every endeavor. The next step in life was, however, the present, and it became the primary force. I also realized how great it was to experience that day in the outdoors and to know that it really was reality. There was no turning back. I was now a trapper. I was what I had dreamed about since I was old enough to push down the spring on a number one long-spring with my foot. I was about to embark upon something I had convinced myself many times that I could never do. Now I knew that dreams could happen and seemingly impossible things could come to pass.

The day in late October finally came when I felt it was time to dig steel into the ground. It was a pre-planned date. I felt the fur

Tracks in the Mud

was prime, and it was a Monday, which meant all the weekend warriors were back to work or school, and I could quietly and methodically go about my work. I remember it as a very wet fall. Not what a dirt-trapper yearns for. Many field roads were too wet to drive, and so I had to walk much more than would normally be necessary. The wet ground also necessitated carrying dry dirt to bed the traps properly. I don't believe it bothered me a bit to walk a quarter or half mile to my set locations. I just put the stuff into my pack basket and set off from the nearest road. The extra time was problematic, but I knew it would dry up eventually, and I would be able to tend the sets by vehicle.

I also remember some of the coyotes I caught that first week. Some sets were on bare earth, and when I came to the trapped coyotes, they looked like huge balls of mud. Their fur was totally caked in mud. Not only were they looking pretty bad, but the weight of carrying the extra soil out to the truck was quite a burden. I had to hose the coyotes off completely with a high pressure stream of water and then dry the critters off in front of fans. It was an extra step, to be certain, but the result was excellent. The finished product was as good as if they had not gotten dirty. My way of thinking was that those coyotes probably had been dirty before and had cleaned up just fine, so why not one more time?

The early coyote trapping wasn't exactly leisurely, but it wasn't the hard-core battle that began with the general water-trapping season. I actually began in daylight and worked until dark. I'd had enough of trapping by flashlight, making sets almost by feel, and looking only for the flash of the eyes of trapped coyotes in the headlights.

The joy of seeking the gray form of the catch lying in the distance gave greater time of excitement and anticipation. The colors and fine detail of the fur in full daylight were like an extra reward. Although there was no time to stand and gloat over each catch, there was less stress to get to the next set location and finish before school. The fall weather, although it was wet at times, still was a beautiful part of the early predator trap line. Most days began with a jacket and often frosty conditions, but some days still ended up with me in shirtsleeves. These were the days that epitomize trapping: the clear cool days, with the land tuning to its mature colors. The crops were ripened, and there was a kind of fullness and satisfaction of all the life on the prairie. Animal populations were at their maximum levels, and food was abundant for both plant eaters as well as the carnivores. The abundance of fall gives the young of the year the sense of ease and quietude. They haven't experienced the sudden changes that would occur in just weeks, and now the land and animals were in a state of complacency. I knew better, but the feeling for a moment was soft and inviting. Fall lulls and tranquilizes all who experience it.

 For me it was a time to get the bugs out of my operation, to gain strength and stamina for the real test to come. Now I operated behind locked gates, on private land, with no apparent competition. It was the time to gain ease and a comfortable feel for being and working in the outdoors all day long. The mindset became one much like that of my quarry. Each day was given to me in its basic form. The weather, the length of the daylight, the geography, the status of the crops in the fields—all were beyond my control. I took what I was given each day and worked with it. Sometimes it worked in favor of me, the hunter, and other times it worked in favor of the hunted. When predators are the game, one sometimes doesn't really know which is which.

 The mornings and the evenings were always the most memorable. Often I would top a hill that overlooked set locations. There I would pause and know that it was only me and the land. There were no politics, no economic policies, no meetings or confrontations—only me and the endless hills running with the gray ghosts whose song echoed in the valleys. There was no blame game here. If I did it right I won. If my truck was empty at the end of the day, there was no one else to blame but me. I couldn't fault the critters, for they only did what they were born to do. If I didn't intercept their inner instincts and extend a steel handshake, they would run past me every time. This time of the season was the essence of the game. I would soon grapple with the more human side of the occupation. Soon I would hit the public areas with the opening of the general water trapping season. For now I enjoyed the quietude. It was all it could be and it was as good as I had expected.

Chapter 13
"Heavy Lifting"

I RAN THE HILLS AS LONG AS PLANNED. I felt that I had a leg up on the season with some nice prime coyotes on the stretchers, but I knew the real money was running the creek bottoms. On schedule I pulled the coyote steel on the dry land. I would return to these locations later to take the long-traveling coyotes that ranged the hills and hollows in search of winter food. Now I must focus on the abundant raccoon population in the process of fattening for the winter along the streams and in the cropland. Timing was everything and, as the 'coon season opened at the beginning of November, I knew that the patterns would change quickly as the corn and milo crop was harvested.

I immediately set all the prospected trails that led in and out of fields. Of course the activity in the shallow streams was heavy as the racoons fed on the abundant food in the water. Public rights of way and bridge locations were set as rapidly as I could get it done. I began at midnight of opening day. Since there were no closed hours for trapping, I wanted to get the greatest jump on the competition

Tracks in the Mud

on these public areas. My experience at night trapping, gained during the previous years, came in very handy. All my locations were pre-determined, and I could set these in the dark if I had to.

I've always thought it was good I had no one to take photos of me on the 'coon trap line. With my muddy sweatshirt, shoulder-length rubber gloves, and hip boots hung from my belt I probably looked pretty awful. Top that off with a headlamp pinned to a dirty hat and a handgun strapped to my side, and I suppose I rivaled some criminal on the loose in appearance. I remember popping over the bank of a stream and finding another trapper there in the dark one night. He caught me in the beam of his light and a very scared look crossed his face. I couldn't figure out why he left the place in such a hurry. Now that I think back about it, I might not have appeared to be the cosiest thing to encounter in the dark.

These were the days of heavy lifting, so to speak. I ran as hard and fast as I could go, driving rapidly from location to location. Many miles were covered each day. My mileage logs showed that a hundred miles a day was pretty average. I'd pull up at a location, jump out of the truck, slide down the bank, remove the catch, reset, and hike back up to the road. The routine was repeated many tims in a day.

I worked into a two-day line, running east one day and then west the next. There was competition now as fur prices were high and every one seemed to want to cash in on the fur boom. I got the best set locations on many streams because I had pre-prospected and knew the best banks and the best trails. If other trappers were working the same area, I "down-streamed" their sets, thereby intercepting the racoon before they reached the sets of the competition. Racoons tended to work upstream, against the current, as they searched for food, so usually the downstream location was best. I suppose the idea for the searching raccoon was to be searching in clear water, rather than in the muddy churned up water downstream from where they'd just walked. There were trappers everywhere, so even if I got to a location first it would probably be set by others. I took the attitude that all the fur was wild and free until it shook hands with my steel. The one to make the catch was the one who won. This wasn't recreational sport-type trapping. It did have its moments though. I met some of the competition, and they were mostly pretty good guys. Amazingly, I ran into very few other trappers, most keeping to themselves and running fast and with little socialization.

I took no lunch breaks or time to rest. I ate a sandwich while I drove and had a swig of water to wash it down. Sometimes I didn't even take the shoulder-length rubber gloves off between locations, since that took extra time. I tried to wash the gloves off in the muddy stream before getting back into the truck, but of course the steering wheel and the inside of the truck did get a bit rank at times. Trapping was a muddy, bloody, smelly operation, but the results were good. I was taking the cream of the crop from public areas and saving the great private locations for later. These private areas were kind of my ace in the hole. It also felt good to be competing in the public areas and coming out pretty well. I piled the raccoon in front of the fans to dry before skinning each night and felt confident I could reach my goals.

I really got into a routine of skinning 'coon. I got to the point where I could skin an average one in less than five minutes. I made sure the fur was perfectly dry before putting them into the freezer. Again, there was a certain efficiency in handling only raccoon. I just kept my hip boots on and systematically hung the critters on my skinning gambrel and pulled the hides off. It was always nice to get done and have a bit of family time in the evening. Operating in two directions always brought me home each night, and I was glad to have such good trapping territory near our home. I talked to a few people sleeping in their trucks having stopped when they were too tired to continue. I was happy I didn't have to do that.

After a couple of weeks of this crazy running, I was happy to have a deep freezer full of racoon fur, but was also glad to welcome the mink, muskrat, and beaver season. The raccoon were now thinned out near the roads and also were changing their habits some as the shallow bits of water were beginning to freeze and the crops were being taken from the fields. The tactic now was to concentrate on muskrats on the state lakes and larger stock ponds in the area. Again I would set the public areas first. This was critical, since the muskrat population would be taken quite quickly by whoever set an area first.

There was a good crop of muskrats on the waterways, and I also had drawn a state lake to trap exclusively by permit. I believed that muskrats would sell at least at the five-dollar mark. I felt that at that price more money could be made trapping muskrats than any other fur. The numbers were fairly high, and I knew I could take good numbers if I got the right places tied up and trapped hard.

The plan was simple: get to the best paces first and set them tight. I had a lot of traps and knew it was a numbers game. The person with the most sets in the water got the most 'rats. Again, it was a midnight opening for me. I had prospected the lakes so well that I knew where all the runways and den entrances were, and I set Conibears in these areas in the dark with very little difficulty. I literally felt my way along the shore line and set the runs with very little help from the light I carried. I had two large lakes set up completely before daylight broke. I continued to set the whole next day. In the meantime I checked a lot of sets and took fur. I used the multiple-catch boxes and a lot of 110 Conibears. Some of the locations had a lot of houses and feed beds, and I set these natural locations as well. All my effort was on the large public lakes where I knew the competition would be and I knew I needed to be there first.

The first few days were a blur. I piled up hundreds of muskrats the first few days of the season, skinned and froze skins when I could get it done, and slept very little. This was the time to catch fur. It could be stretched later. I knew of some trappers who froze their muskrat catch whole without even skinning them, but I just didn't have enough freezer space to be able to do that. The weather was good and I knew the competition would be relentless. I never really stopped to count, but I felt I was making the best money I had ever made in my life. I guess the adrenaline kept pumping for those first days of the season. Sure, sometimes I felt I met myself coming when I was going. Someone saw me at a lake and commented he had seen me at another lake earlier that day and was wondering if I was twins. This was the most profitable part of the season but also the most grueling. I knew I needed to make the effort, but I also knew I couldn't keep it up indefinitely.

The exposure to theft was great, and I felt I should be every where all the time to monitor my sets. It was hard for me to just write off trap and fur theft. I remember many times when I made a new set, I came to find the area all torn up, the result of a catch, and then I saw the trap set back not in a way I had left it. Of course the catch had been stolen. To top it off someone had tried to re-set the trap to make it appear no catch had been made. Having traps just plain stolen was also a problem. The tell-tale footprints would give it away and of course that empty feeling would be there. I could never get used to that feeling. It took away from the trapping experience. I just had to look at the catch at the end of the day and be positive about what I had and realize that it was profitable and go on. I became a

Tracks in the Mud

bit hardened and finally just took the fur that I could and moved on. I don't attribute theft and harassment as much to other trappers as to passersby, ignorant so-called outdoorsmen, and anti-fur harvest fanatics. My consolation was that the best was yet to come, because I had a lot of private land to work. The other thing was that the fair weather trappers would soon be gone. Most would move on to watching football or go deer hunting, and I would have the land more or less to myself and a few other hardcore trappers who just wanted to make their catches and bother no one else.

I had lots of private lakes and my permit lake to trap also. I had to think about the weather at this point since it was the middle of November and I needed to harvest the fur off the private areas as well. Cold weather could at this point really make it hard to do a good job on my private lands. After a week of hitting the public areas very hard, I pulled most of the steel and went to my exclusive areas. It was a pleasant change to be sure. Again I felt I had a good leg up by having taken a lot of public "up-for-grabs" fur first, and now I could systematically harvest the fur from my private areas. Being on private land and my exclusive permit area really was a luxury. It was kind of like fighting a guerilla war and then retreating to a protected area. I could trap in the daylight and set areas, harvest them, and then move on in a sane fashion. It was really good to have a little breathing room. I felt human again and even saw my wife and daughter a bit more. Again, my wife was my best cheering section and supported me so wonderfully in this endeavor.

Chapter 14

"Pure Nirvana, Good Bucks, and a Break"

I IMAGINE AT THIS TIME IN THE LATE 1970s that a helicopter flight over the plains of Nebraska during November might find more activity in the pre-dawn morning than one might imagine. Far below upon the grid of mile section roads, headlights would travel in squares, tracing the perimeters of sections in a stop-and-go pattern. If the light of the day began to break, one would notice that the sporadic stops of vehicles coincided with the intersections of waterways and fence-lines.

The aerial reporter would wonder at the meaning of all the activity, yet if they knew the patterns of the land and the trails of furbearers, they would begin to get the story. Such flights of reporters, if they had occurred, would have landed in harvested fields and stopped the drivers of pickup trucks to get the up-to-the minute interviews. The ramblings of all manner of colorful characters would have split the airwaves, in a most remarkable manner.

Since such reports never took place, I guess that at this time a bit of comment is warranted regarding the trapping community in

Tracks in the Mud

general. In the late seventies, trappers were beginning to really come out of the woodwork. Every place where some type of water intersected with a roadway, I would find truck tracks where a vehicle had pulled off the roadway and stopped. There were always the telltale hip-boot tracks in the gravel or dirt. Some places were more popular than others, and there would be a trail of packed-down grass where people had gone down to the water. Boot tracks in the mud along the stream banks led to various traps set mostly for 'coon. Signs of competition were everywhere.

The so-called space-age trapper had arrived. It was a subculture to which I belonged. As I look back, I see it more than I did at the time. We were a very mobile and production-oriented breed of trapper. It's still true today in the next century. I think we were the real beginning of the truly long-line trapper. We covered lots of territory and took good numbers of fur. Certainly the old bridge-trapping "minkers" in Minnesota and other areas had the concept figured out long before. No more were trappers content to just trap their home farm or a lake or two near home. They ranged out into other areas to multiply the catch. I suppose I was too busy just trapping to make ends meet to think about which group of working Americans I belonged to. Most of the trappers came from some type of trapping heritage. Either they had grown up setting a few traps with their fathers or siblings, or they had an uncle or grandfather who trapped. The fur boom of the seventies and eighties revived the tradition among families that had some history on the trap line. There were a lot of people who were doing it pretty full time. Many who did seasonal work trapped in the fall and winter months. Some took vacation time from their regular jobs and trapped during these days. There were a few who would even migrate to other states to trap as the seasons opened farther south and the conditions in the northern states became tougher because of the weather. Some took trapping vacations just like folks now are inclined to go to South Dakota pheasant hunting. People would go to New Mexico to trap bobcats and coyotes. Trappers traversed the roads and waterways in record numbers in these years, and yet the average person knew little of the industry going on right under their nose.

I met many kinds of trappers. Some were folks who had trapped a lot for as long as they could remember. They simply extended their trap lines and replicated what they had done for years, only in a larger area. Some, of course had been long-line mink trappers who read the fur market and concentrated on the fur that was most profitable.

There were some, like me, who had trapped since they were kids, who now because of their circumstance could do it full time and fulfill a dream. Some also bought fur, sold trapping supplies and did other types of wild-crafting activities to make a living. I met one guy who trapped all fall and winter, helped a local fur buyer handle fur, and also worked for him at buying fur. One of his jobs was to peddle low-grade furs to other fur buyers so his employer's average grade of fur would be higher. As a buyer, a trapper didn't want to see him unloading fur at his place, unless he could make money on low-grade furs. His summers were spent working on local farms. Another guy was the epitome of the fur entrepreneur, who invested in lots of traps and equipment and actually hired people to run trap lines for him. He trained them and laid out the areas they were to work. Since most trappers were very individualistic, this was much the exception to the typical trapper, who worked alone or with a partner. My guess is that he had a large turnover of workers, as they set out on their own.

I ran into another young guy while I was out on the trap line. He had graduated from high school and had never set a trap before.

He'd bought some books and equipment and was trapping full time for the first time. It sounded like he was getting a lot of on-the-job training. His catch wasn't extraordinary, but he was apparently paying his expenses and keeping the gas tank full. In addition, there were retired guys supplementing their Social Security checks with a fur check. Some of these fellows put on some incredible miles and gave great credibility to the concept of trapping smart and not hard. I wished I had their knowledge of the trap line. With youth and knowledge, one could have gone very far. The old saying of my grandfather really rang true. He said, "Too soon old, too late smart." I had an old bachelor neighbor, who trapped a lot of 'coon each fall and all he did was drive up to all the old abandoned buildings in the area and set live traps in them. As the weather turned cold and drove the raccoon to better shelter, he took many racoons. Often he had the farmers who lived there just check the traps and give him a call when he had made a catch. I remember seeing his old Chevy pickup go by every day as he went around and picked up his furs.

    Besides all the full- and part-time trappers, some very serious about making all or part of their living from the trap line, there were the kids. I saw them as I traveled the countryside—grade school and junior high students. Most were farm boys who walked down to the nearest creek and wired a number one Victor to a log or tree stump in hope of catching an unsuspecting raccoon or mink. Some of them I would see as I passed their homes at early hours of the morning, sneaking down the front steps, flashlight in hand wearing a pair of hip boots. Some of them I only recognized by the sets they made, usually uncovered traps with pans set high and traps not bedded very securely into the soil. I wondered if they had the eternal optimism I remembered having at that age. I envisioned them faithfully checking those sets every morning, and each time they held the same high hopes for a catch. For them, like me, the thrill was always in the anticipation of the new day. I suppose these kids fancied themselves driving four-wheel-drive trucks around the countryside, piling up volumes of high-priced fur and making a fine living from the life of a trapper. They knew little about the fur boom they were in, nor much of the fickle volatility of the high fur market they thought was the "norm." Sometimes one of these young fur harvesters would be walking down a gravel road with a fine muskrat grasped by the tail, and I could see their joy and pride. No one could take away the self-esteem they had earned with that catch.

As I got into late November, I really appreciated being in Nebraska. Although the weather could get severe at this time, it also settled down and gave some nice days. There were days when I could still work with little more than a sweatshirt, and the water was still relatively ice-free. I began to put a few dirt sets in at strategic locations and this mixed up my trapping day as well as my catch. I used dry dirt and anti-freeze to keep the sets from freezing up during the frosty nights, but it really wasn't much of an inconvenience. Now I could run a fairly mixed trap line since I was operating mostly on private land and I felt it was efficient to take all the types of fur.

I felt I could actually stop and eat a sandwich for lunch. It became pleasant to find a scenic spot to eat. Often I would stop on a hill top where the panorama of the fall prairie would stretch out to the horizon. I'd scout the rolling hills and imagine where the best set locations would be for the various furbearers that ran that area. I even began to notice the sounds. Pheasants crowed and waterfowl announced their migration as they passed overhead. This was the kind of trapping I imagined when I was a youngster dreaming of the trap line. Now there were the special sets in the spring-holes where one could pick up a nice buck mink or a pair of 'coons. There were

Tracks in the Mud

always muskrats mixed into the catch, which paid the gas bills and then some. The land sets yielded some prime coyotes and an occasional fox. There were always surprises now. The mink caught in a dry set Conibear, the double on racoon in a pair of snares, or the beautiful prime badger in a dirt hole set.

Each day I set new areas and moved sets to better locations. There was always the excitement of checking new areas for the first time, and it kept the endeavor fresh and full of wonder. It became a routine of new experiences each day. My days were now experienced in full daylight and that made it a real joy to trap. I always had a variety of fur to skin and handle each evening and of course now was the time of the most prime and beautiful fur to be caught. Trapping had become an almost regular job. Each day I could tally my probable profit and I was working a pretty regular schedule. The beauty was that my route and timing were my own, and I made my own schedule. I could be home at a reasonable hour and even spend some evening time with the family. This was a good time.

By Thanksgiving we decided we should sell some fur. The market sounded strong. In retrospect we could have waited and maybe got more money for that early fur, but it was good to know we had made some money in the bank. We were very happy with the prices and it certainly encouraged a strong effort in the latter part of the season. A bit of a break to sell fur and celebrate Thanksgiving was also appreciated.

The trap line now hopped from farm to farm, hitting the hot pockets of fur activity, centered around open springs and the best crossings where the coyotes traveled in their long winter loops. There were lakes with some clear ice on them which meant some good opportunity for muskrat trapping, and the beaver trapping also lent another dimension to the early winter. Heading toward the holiday season brought some snows and also some thaws. The 'coon were still active and all the fur was of the most excellent quality. I knew that my next lot of fur would bring top dollar. I also had time to stretch and finish most of the fur I caught and that would make for a nice trip to the fur buyers for bids.

The almost predictable frequency of storm fronts sweeping through the state made for real patterns of fur catches. It was important to keep all the sets working and then sit out a bad day to run the next day and dig lots of prime fur out of the snow drifts.

Christmas break was a time to pull up sets and take a bit of time off. We would go to Minnesota to visit family and would also incorporate fur selling into the vacation. It was good to talk to friends and relatives, get a picture of the trapping scene in Minnesota, and swap stories and fur prices. My wife had off during Christmas and New Year's and it made for a good break. I was anxious, however, to get back out on the trap line, and right at the beginning of January I set out to put in some traps and snares.

Chapter 15

"The Frosting on the Cake and Kill-Dogs on the Prairie"

A SENSE OF QUIETUDE SETTLED UPON the trap line after Christmas. There weren't so many trappers left out there. The easy fur was all gone. The real money had been made, but I figured anything I took now was the frosting on the cake. Competition was down, and I still had places to go. I decided when expenses exceeded income, it would be time to quit.

There were still some beaver colonies that needed attention, and I quickly found that, in the moving water near the dams, other fur congregated. Muskrats fed on the mud banks, racoons still entered the open water, and of course the mink also found these areas attractive. I was surprised at the amount of fur yet to be taken in these areas. Water trapping was still profitable.

It was the cable snare that saved me on the coyote line. It was getting tough to tie up the wary old dogs in steel traps, but the snow led me to many great crossings that allowed me to tie them up with snares. I had learned how to hang snares from an expert snaresman. He taught me the loop size and how to make a great lock from bent washers. I bought cable and crimps and was in business for little money. From there it was just a matter of using common sense of where coyotes moved through the countryside. It got back to the old concept of trail-setting, getting to know the animal on the most intimate level, knowing where it would put its head and neck. It was a marvelous concept. A coyote roamed many miles on the average night, but somehow I needed to get him to put his head through a fourteen-inch loop of cable. It was hard to make a critter go where they didn't want it to go. Snaring was an exercise in cooperation. I just had to let him do what he was going to do and be there with the snare when he did it.

Up close and personal with a fox.

Tracks in the Mud

Each day I counted my fur: some days a few beaver and some 'rats, and maybe a mink. Other days there would be a couple of prime coyotes and a couple of 'coons. Not huge money, but wages above expenses, and so the month of January pulled me through. By the end of the month, I again had a nice assortment of fur to sell. The water fur was still excellent, and the coyotes were still in good shape. I knew they would start to rub soon. I didn't want to kill them if they weren't in good condition. The coyotes were starting to get worked pretty hard by both hunters and trappers, and I didn't want the resource to be depleted. The lowly coyote went from a hated predator, due no respite from persecution, to a valuable fur animal. There were those who began to call for its protection as a furbearer. Mostly it was trappers who wanted to set a season on them and protect them during the summer months. It's amazing how people will protect an animal that has value. The best thing for a species was for it to have economic value. Then it will be protected and people will look out for its best interest.

There were some good coyote trappers in Nebraska, but the hunters really hit the predators hard as well. Of course everyone in the rural areas had a rifle in the cab of their truck, loaded and ready for any coyote that made the mistake of showing up near a road at the wrong time. Interestingly, at the time it was illegal to have a loaded shotgun in the car, but rifles could be loaded. This was, I believe, a concession to farmers and ranchers who demanded to be ready to eliminate coyotes whenever possible. When the first snow arrived, lots of coyotes would be shot, since they now showed up well. Folks got a lot of shots from vehicles. Besides a few callers, the drive and spot method was employed by a lot of hunters.

The dog hunters were probably the most deadly breed of coyote hunter and they were indeed a special breed. Most would have a pack of running dogs of the greyhound type. These hounds were long-legged and had incredible stamina to run for miles. When a fresh track was found or an unlucky coyote crossed a road and they saw it, the trail dogs were released. They would run the coyote which would usually circle. These hunters seemed to have an instinct for where the coyote would come out or cross a road. They would be there and when the coyote crossed the road, they would release the "kill-dogs" which were a pair of fierce dogs that could run fast for a short time. They would quickly overtake the coyote and kill it very quickly. These dogs worked in pairs and got on either side of the coyote and probably broke its neck. The "kill-dogs" hunted by sight and seemed to key in on the movement of the coyote. I heard stories to the effect, that these dogs would sometimes attack trail dogs that were following too close to quarry. The killers were definitely not the type of dog anyone would want to go running out in front of. I don't know what kind of fur quality was attained with this method, but guys with good dogs killed a lot of coyotes. The ranchers liked to see the coyote numbers thinned out, and theses hunters seemed to achieve the goal.

There were also guys who had dogs that merely trailed the coyotes until they could get a shot with a rifle, and these guys also seemed to do pretty well.

The pressure on the coyote population became very great during these years. I was always amazed at how the species not only survived but thrived under such pressure. Each season there was a good population to harvest. Coyotes became more cunning as a result of the relentless pressure, and they also stayed healthy, with less incidence of mange and other canine diseases.

By the end of January, I felt I had done a pretty good job of harvesting most of the fur in my area. There was still breeding stock, and

I felt confident that a new batch of fur would repopulate my areas. There were a few muskrat spots to set yet, and I was able to size down to a part-time trap line for a couple of weeks. I had other responsibilities to take care of regarding my other business, and I also had odd chores such as pulling coyote stakes that had frozen into the ground. I wanted to be sure to get all my stakes out before farmers got into the fields. I had an interesting stake puller that hooked onto the stake in the ground and had a sliding hammer-weight that could be forcefully slid upward to hammer the stake from frozen ground. I also pre-scouted some areas to see what was left, just to get an idea of the potential for the next season. I tried to get all my equipment cleaned, inventoried and put away.

The season seemed complete. The last fur was marketed and the stakes were all pulled. Late February brought the first exhalations of the South and the wedges of geese now pointed northward. The frosts still came but the arc of the sun grew longer. I knew the trapping season had been all it could be. The cycle had been completed and a dream had been accomplished. It was like graduation from college. Yes, I still had a lot to learn, but the means of learning it was now in place.

Chapter 16

"Summer Wisdom, Eternal Gifts"

SUMMER INTRUDED INTO MARCH and then receded again ahead of frosty nights, but by May summer was much in control and the bustle of school, family, and work engulfed us. Our second child was scheduled to arrive later that summer, and preparation for that event also occupied our time. Yet, since I lived in the country and traveled through the trapping areas each day, thoughts and memories of the trap line danced in my mind. Each time we crossed a creek, I turned as we went over the bridge to see if a muskrat or beaver might be swimming along the bank. As we passed the farms where the tree lines crossed the road, I looked for the perfect coyote location and visualized the travel routes of the canine predators. When we came home at night, we searched the gravel roads for sets of eyes glowing in the headlights, giving away the activities of raccoon families.

Already the process was beginning again as I visited landowners and talked of farming and trapping and other matters of the land. I met farmers stopped in their fields as they tend to mowing or cul-

Tracks in the Mud

tivation. Sometimes we talked for an hour, and our conversation condensed to the basic common sense of those who work outdoors and made a living with their hands and their wits. I thought back now to the countless times I worked out the world's problems, as I stood on the steps of a tractor cab and traded the wisdom of the land with a farmer or rancher. How much better off we all might be if some of these guys were in Washington, I decided. These farmers and ranchers understood economics, foreign policy, and especially conservation. They knew and loved the wildlife and understood the common sense of what a trapper did and what his role was in the overall scheme of wildlife management.

One farmer, upon whose land I trapped coyotes, was happy to have their numbers reduced among his livestock, but he also had no time for the feral dogs that sometimes ran the countryside. His rule for me was not to allow any stray dogs I saw on his property to escape. They didn't belong there and in his opinion were as bad as or worse than coyotes on his livestock. There were rules out here, rules that may not have been popular in some segments of society, but very practical rules, nonetheless.

Feral cats were another issue that brought comment from landowners. Some folks hated the stray cats because they killed so many birds. In reality, cats were a non-native and invasive species. During the fur boom years, a demand for cat skins actually developed, and some buyers actually bought them. I never felt I wanted to get into that trade, since many cat-lovers would find it offensive. Yet these feral cats had little business out in the fields and woodlots, and many landowners were happy to have people rid the landscape of them.

Each season, as I met and visited with landowners, I reviewed their rules and kept notes on important things. Of course, as mentioned earlier, gates were always a big issue. It was always important to keep them as they were found. There were common sense things like not driving on hayfields or not tearing up field roads if they were too wet to be driven upon. Some guys would allow me to trap, but were careful to point out that there would be no hunting, since they reserved that for themselves. I found that hunting really didn't mix with trapping anyway. I never had the time to stop and go after a pheasant or a flock of mallards when I was rushing to get the fur harvest done.

Some farmers wanted all of the muskrats taken from their stock ponds because of how destructive they were on the earth dams. Even if one tried, it was nearly impossible to eradicate them, but surely I kept their numbers under control. Most farmers were pleased to have raccoon numbers reduced, since they were hard on the nests of ground nesting gamebirds such as pheasant and quail and also were destructive to a lot of crops and stored grains.

Fences were also a great concern to a lot of landowners. They worked a lot of hours each year to keep them under repair, and they did not like people carelessly crossing them or doing damage to them. It was good to take the leisurely days of summer to visit with landowners and make sure we were on the same page as far as access to the land was concerned.

As we worked and relaxed during that hot dusty summer, the cooling air of many evenings found us on gravel and dirt roads checking for the tracks of 'coon under bridges or knocking on landowners' doors to visit and confirm trapping permission. The tracks were of mixed sizes now with youngsters following their moms, but the number of smaller tracks gave an indication of future harvest potential, and it seemed as though the fur crop was abundant. A few pretty good rains had kept the water levels up and there was sign that the

Tracks in the Mud

muskrats had faired well in their efforts to propagate the species. We were beginning to hear the yelps of the young coyote pups as the trains rolled by and things were shaping up for a prosperous trapping season. Prices looked strong and inventories on the world market were sold down well.

Gaining trapping permissions involved a lot of driving and knocking on doors. We met a lot of interesting people and often the process of gaining access to land was almost as much enjoyment as the actual harvesting of the fur later in the season. During our years of trapping in Nebraska we spent much time talking to rural folks and sometimes permission became easy, even enjoyable to obtain.

Ronald and Annie Dosinger, for example, had a nice stream flowing through their farm and also some nice travel-ways the coyotes funneled through. We got to know them pretty well over our years in Nebraska. They only lived a couple miles south of us and raised some chickens along with the grain crops and beef cattle. Not only had I found a great trapping place when I first asked permission, but also a source for the freshest eggs around.

Ronald had a perpetual smile on his face, and Annie took an immediate shine to our kids. We traveled there often to get eggs and to visit. I can still hear Ronald say, "Did you hear that thunderstorm the other night? It was a real thrumper."

The eggs never came out of the cooler very fast. "Come on in for coffee. I think Annie just baked some cookies." So the visit began, and two hours later the eggs finally came out of the cooler. "Here's an extra dozen. They're a little small." The dollar-fifty sale was completed in just over two hours. Then the "Big Red" gum came out for the kids.

If the visit was late summer, Ronald would usually say something like, "I suppose pretty soon you'll be setting some coyote traps.

I've been hearing them almost every night. There's some beaver on the creek you should catch before they cut down my fruit trees." Getting permission from Ronald was better than good. We were fed homemade cookies, got the freshest eggs imaginable, and also the assurance that I could trap their land again in the fall.

Our adjacent neighbors were also great. None of them trapped, so they were just fine with allowing a next-door neighbor to trap on their land. I always felt I needed to at least broach the subject, though, and not just take for granted that I could trap their land. Usually they would bring it up during the course of the summer. "So I suppose you'll be trapping again this fall?" I would nod and the deal would be done.

One neighbor pulled up to the house one late summer day, "I hope you get those coyotes thinned out again, there was a whole litter born out by the dump in the back quarter." That was another permission granted with little effort expended.

I remember the neighbor to the east. As I talked to him one day he said, "Lightning hit one of my cows in that pasture just over the hill from your place. I had to get it hauled away quick before the coyotes tore it up."

Later in the summer I was over to his place helping castrate some hogs. "Hold the little squealer steady now," he said as he did his job with the knife. "So I suppose you'll be setting some traps in the pasture pretty soon."

"Yep I plan on it," I said as I let the squirming porker go into the pen.

Rebecca Wallane had to be ninety years old. She was a widow and still lived on the little ranch that had supported her and her late husband for many years. She still burned wood to heat the little house and did all her cooking on a wood stove. White locks of hair protruded from under her straw hat as she tended her vegetable garden, the first time I drove onto the place. She eyed me a bit suspiciously but certainly had no fear to let me know she lived alone out there. She looked too tough to worry about anything. The skin of her face and arms had come to almost match the late-summer hues of the rangeland behind her home, yet her eyes were clear and bright like the moonlight on a pristine lake. Her old cattle dog was a blue-heeler, blind in one eye, so when he barked at me, he always turned to one side so he could see who he was antagonizing.

There's no doubt she had opinions and I soon learned she was brought up Baptist and would die the same. "Not Southern Baptist, they went way off the deep end long ago," she told me. "No, I'm just plain Bible-believin' Baptist."

Of course I was interested in a section of land that she owned. It was high and rolling, so the sky met it at the other end. There were stock ponds that held the goodness of spring rain on the land and windmills that still filled stock tanks. I also had noticed the many coyote tracks and droppings in the dusty earth where the cow trails met the sorting corrals.

"You know that pasture has never been broke. There're still prickly pears in there, and you know the cattle always eat the native grasses first before anything that's been planted." She went on to tell me of the land, how it greened up and fed cattle and how in the Thirties it nearly blew away, "The prairie here held the soil while lots of cropland blew to Ioway."

It took awhile, but I found she had no great love for coyotes. "I've fought 'em for as long as we've been here. They'll take calves you know."

Finally she said, "If you trap, mind the gates, and if you hunt watch the cattle."

Permission granted. I had some great times on that place, tying down doubles on young coyotes and taking muskrats from the stock ponds. I even remember some limits of doves shot over those water holes. The greatest times were the visits when my wife and I stopped to see her. She invited us in to see her pictures, and we smelled the fresh-bread baking in the wood-burning oven. She was a tireless lady, and it would seem she still must be hoeing her garden and splitting wood to this day. She is eternally etched upon my memory.

In the middle of August our son was born. Much-needed rain marked the occurrence, and we had only a little time to adjust our lives to two children before my wife's school began, and I finished my early fall work and began to concentrate on the trapping season, which was rapidly approaching.

It's hard to define the feelings that accompany a child being born, but of course the thoughts of continuity and passing the torch become paramount. Now my mind linked that old rusty number one trap, which I had set as a youngster, to my newborn son. I wondered if he too would be bitten by the urge to wander around the hills and streams wearing hip boots and dirty hooded-sweatshirts. I wondered if he would someday lose some of the traps I now set in these streams and fields. I thought little of fur markets or changing world attitudes about fur. I wondered mostly if I would be able to somehow pass along the incredible mystery and the amazing wonder of sets of tracks in mud or of a hair caught in a fence. Could I convey how these tiny remnants, linked to a world of intermingled ecosystems, somehow connected to people like us, who learned to know these signs and then interjected our lives into the instincts of the wild. A whole new perspective opens when the things a person loves and believes since childhood appear in one's life. Now there is an urgency to find ways to link these to children, and by so doing to focus them upon the infinite future.

As a new trapping season began it was not merely an opportunity to do what I enjoyed and earn some income, but a challenge to make it a better and more sustainable thing. I didn't just want the dream for me, but also for them. Most of all, I guess I felt they needed to always know that their dreams could be realized and their dreams were important. I could never stifle my children's aspirations with what I believed to be some perceived practicality. I now began to link the importance of accomplishing our goals to the essence of life.

Packing up furs ready to ship to market.

Chapter 17

"A Lucky Split and New Horizons"

*I*T WAS AN EARLY SEPTEMBER DAY, the temperature in the low nineties, and I was thinking how hot it must be in the classroom since my wife had just started back to school. The leaves on the cottonwoods sparkled as the wind caused them to flutter hysterically.

I was on a pasture near our home. Today I practiced. Yes the major preparations were done, the traps were ready, permissions had been obtained, and now I felt the urge to actually put steel into the ground.

I suppose it's a lot like gardening. Gardeners can plan all winter but it's not until a spade is put into the earth that one really arrives at the goal. So it now seemed time to put a spade into the earth, literally. With cicadas droning in the green trees and the hot sun beating down, I pushed my trapping spade into the soil. I had brought my pack basket with a trap and stake, my dirt-sifter and hammer. I even brought bottles of lure and coyote urine. I dug the hole and excavated a trap-bed. I placed the trap into the bed and firmly packed it in so it could not be moved by a misplaced coyote foot. I then completed the set by sifting dirt over the set trap. The stake had been driven into the hard dirt and the set was finished with the proper lure and urine. I stepped back and looked at the completed coyote set. It looked good. I couldn't resist taking the handle of the trapping shovel and tapping it on the manufactured coyote track over the trap-pan. The jaws came up through the covering and gripped the shovel-handle. Dirt flew and my skin tingled with excitement. This would have to keep the trapping fever at bay for a bit longer, but practice did make perfect and it never hurt to make sure I had the nuts and bolts of the business down.

I looked now at the fall season as a "can do" thing. I knew where the fur was, my permissions were in place and my equipment was in the final stages of being readied. I waited only for the official trapping regulations to come out so I could plan the specifics of dates and times and places.

As often happens, "plan A" can be changed by unforseen circumstances, and so it happened that the Game and Parks Commission, in its constant endeavor to manage fur resources better, changed some important laws. The State of Nebraska decided, in the interest of better quality fur, to divide the state into north and south trapping zones. The north zone would open about ten days earlier than the south zone. All of my trapping areas lay in the south zone, but we really lived very close to the line. It soon occurred to me that there must be some kind of opportunity for me resulting from the law changes. It could mean a longer time period to trap early coyotes, since I would not have to start on 'coon as early, but as I looked at fur prices I realized that with raccoon selling in the forty dollar range, that was the fur where the best money was to be made.

My best option, it seemed, was to establish a 'coon line in the area north of the dividing line. That would mean I would have two opening shots at the raccoon. I could set the opening and run hard for ten days in the north zone, and then set the south zone opening and run hard there. My main trapping territory would be closed while I ran traps in the north zone and creamed off some fur I wouldn't otherwise have been able to get. The only drawback was that I'd have a bit less time to spend on the early coyotes before the opening of the raccoon season in the north zone.

Armed with good maps and notebooks, I set out to prospect a trap line in the north trapping zone. I looked for areas that had the greatest abundance of creeks and other water-features, doing the preliminary work by looking at the maps. Finally I settled on an area to the north and east of our home, where the complex maze of creeks drained into the Platte and Missouri rivers. My first sets weren't all that far from home, and I developed a loop that took me through some great raccoon country and ended up not too far from home. I would be mainly trapping roadside right-of-ways and other public areas. The whole trap line was designed as a quick in-and-out kind of operation. My plan, was to set the line, run it intensively, and pull out to set my home areas in the south zone when it opened ten days later. It took a week of prospecting in early October, but I had every set mapped out and knew exactly what it would take to get the job done.

Another law change that affected me that season was kind of a good news/bad news change. All state lakes would now be legal for all trappers to harvest fur, and there would be no drawing for exclusive rights to trap a certain lake. The bad news was that I would have no chance to get an exclusive permit, but the good news was that I could now trap all of the lakes. I needed to scout all the lakes for the best potential fur numbers. I wanted to be at the best places first when the muskrat and mink season opened. It would require a

Tracks in the Mud

more intense and hectic schedule at the beginning of the general water-trapping season, yet with enough traps and some long hours, I felt I could take some good numbers of fur. By knowing the laws and planning, I also had the element of surprise going for me, since some trappers seemed to buy their license and read the laws about a day before the season. I was ready and well prepared for the state lake trapping run. It reminded me a bit more of the competitive battle we waged each opening day in Minnesota to set up the public lakes and waterways.

I recall this season as one of the best, not only in terms of amounts of fur caught, but also because of great fur prices and, just plain good organization and fairly cooperative weather. There was no question now if trapping full time was a good decision. I knew we could accomplish our goals. The fur crop was out there like the ripening grain in a farmer's field. All I needed to do was to properly connect the dots: do the right things at the right time, and good results should fall into place. Of course there were always the risk factors with any business, but I knew that the weather and competition could be overcome by planning and hard work.

As the fall weather fronts began to sweep across the plains, each one dropping colder air and being followed by frost, the new season began to unfold. The subtle browning of the landscape, the red rows of maturing grain sorghum fields, and the settling of the streams into fall quiescence, greeted my anticipation of the new fur season.

As the first fur primed, I set coyote traps. The weather was dry and cooperative, and the bunched-up coyote families gave generously to our family fund. The spirit of the prairie wolfer filled my days, and I was tempted to roll to the horizon on coyote pelts and forgo the early 'coon season in the north fur zone. Fortunately, I

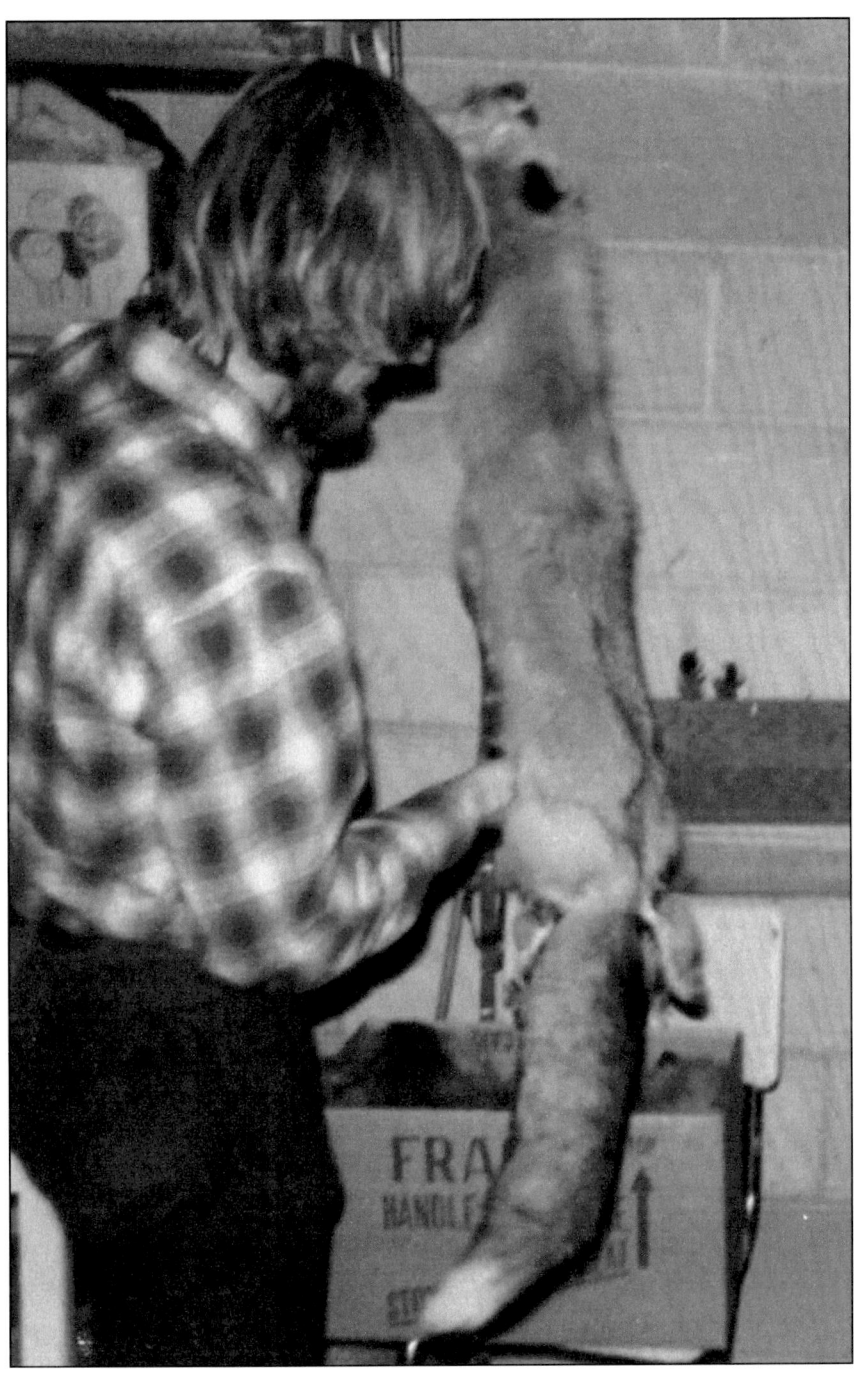
Prime red fox were a prized commodity during the great fur boom.

Tracks in the Mud

didn't give in to the temptation and followed the plan I had formulated before the season and pulled the coyote steel to begin the 'coon season on my north trap line.

I didn't start at midnight, but I did arrive at the first set location well before daylight. I could set the spot in the dark, for it was a point that was burned into my memory. There was a trail with countless racoon tracks that turned past a steep bank just down steam from where a bridge crossed the road. It was perfect for a couple of pocket sets, and the steep bank would hide the set from view from the road. I had planned as many of the sets as possible to be hidden from view. With my five-gallon bucket in hand, filled with traps, stakes, and bait, I bounded down the bank to the water. There was no sign any other trapper had been there, and I quickly put in my sets. The weather was still pretty warm, and bare hands made the setting quicker and easier. To someone who grew up in the water-rich trapping areas of Minnesota, there is always a special thrill to be out in hip-boots and setting the steel in the waterways.

The quietude of the pre-dawn, the humid smells of maturing crops, and the reflection of fallen leaves in the lamp-lit stream were still indelibly etched into my memory. So the day embraced me, it wrapped its powerful arms around me and swept me from set-location to set-location. The strength of such a task, which totally encapsulates one's mind and body and carries one along in its timelessness and rush of excitement, is beyond words. The trap line motivated all the senses, and a day such as this filled the sight with extra perception, as every mark in the mud was a tip-off of the previous night's activity. The smells gave meaning to each step in the musky mud, and every brush with the mellowing grasses. The sounds of water passing over a bridge apron or the whipping sound of supple willows near the water's edge, marked locations and indeed marked the day as one of a kind. The feeling of the silt on my hands, roughened by the cold water and constant depressing of trap-springs was scratched into my memory. Infinite feelings and memories were compressed into such a day.

It was two o'clock before I even thought of the lunch I'd packed. I worked around the loop of dirt and gravel roads, taking side excursions to particularly good-looking spots, and marking all my sets on maps coordinated with notes in my notebook. The pile of traps in the back of the truck dwindled, and as I set I constantly reviewed the sets made and anticipated the catches that should greet me on the next morning.

I arrived home after dark, with a muddy face and river slime caked on my boots. It took a lot of hose action and scrubbing to lighten my load of silt. I was tired but had amazed even myself with the number of sets put in during one day.

This was a night to relax but much anticipate the next day and gloat over the work done. Tonight there was no skinning, no preparation, only the anticipation of jumping into a truck with only my setting tools and my handgun strapped to my belt. As tired as I was, I still fought sleep by allowing the sets to play in my mind to tease me with their perfection. Each set had the potential to make a catch, each one enticed me to review its construction and potential.

Exhaustion was the best sleeping pill in the world, however, and even the excitement of the first night of a new season could not stave off sleep. But 3:00 a.m. came quickly enough, and I was ready. I was in constant wonder of what kept the excitement so new, what caused each season to create the same energy. I could hardly wait to shine my light into the first set location. There was nothing like the beginning of the water-trapping season to someone who has been sloshing around in the late fall lakes and streams for as long as he could remember.

There would be the flash of eyes in the light, down the bank, re-make the set, shake the water from the 'coon's fur, and put the catch into the back of the truck. This was a routine repeated many times during the next days. I'd see the puff of gray in the tall grass, signaling a dead 'coon in a Conibear. There were the new sets, traps moved each day to better locations and little extensions of the trap line. Some days ended late, in the basement, skinning raccoons, storing the harvest in the freezers. Each day I felt I was taking a bonus catch, trapping a new area that I could not have done if it were not for the change in the law. This was the only year the State of Nebraska did the split season. A lot of the complaints came from trappers who worked the northern areas exclusively. I suppose they felt pressure from people who moved in from the southern zone.

Running this extra trap line in another area did some things to broaden my horizons. I learned that one could go into an area cold, with nothing but maps and a notebook and put together a successful trap line. It was a very fulfilling feeling to forge a completely new trap line and have success at it. It was like getting a large gift, one not expected and adding it to your account. It was like getting the frosting on the cake first. So I hit the area hard, pulled my traps in time to re-set in my own area and came away with a nice batch of raccoon fur without sacrificing any of my own fur in my home areas. I was much encouraged to expand into other areas and lengthen my trap lines after this experience. I did return to this trap line on other occasions even though the whole state opened its trapping season at the same time.

Another thing that broadened my fur adventuring horizons occurred one morning while checking traps during the early 'coon season. I had just checked some sets and was getting into my truck when a neighboring farmer pulled up by my truck. He noted that I must be a trapper. We talked a bit about the weather and the raccoon population. Soon he asked me what racoon fur was selling for. I said I hadn't really sold any yet, but I heard prices were pretty decent. Finally he asked me to take a look at a raccoon he had killed in his yard the evening before. Of course it was not skinned and had been shot, but otherwise seemed in good condition. He said he really didn't want to take it to a fur buyer and wondered if I'd be interested in buying it. I told him I wasn't a fur buyer and really didn't want to buy his racoon. Besides, I carried little cash and had no checkbook. After he asked a couple more times, I finally dug a ten-spot out of my pocket. It was about all I had. He seemed happy to make the trade and not to have to bother with the critter anymore. I threw it into my pile of raccoon in the back of the truck.

Later that night as I skinned my catch, I noted that the one I had traded for a ten dollar bill was about as good as any of the others I had trapped. I also noted later in the season that the racoon I had acquired for ten dollars that day on the trap line sold at the same average as the others, and I realized that I had more than quadrupled my ten dollar bill. It didn't take a business wizard to see that money could be made buying fur.

I had gotten to know a lot of fur buyers over the years and many of them bought dealer lots of fur. I also knew that when I had large lots of fur to sell, there was bargaining power to push the price up a bit. I talked to some of the buyers I felt were pretty honest guys, and they encouraged me to do some buying. I usually sold my fur out of state because the local buyers in Nebraska rarely paid what I could get when I went to other dealers. I also knew that I could easily pay what other buyers were paying for in-carcass animals, then skin, finish, and stretch them and realize a really good profit for that extra work. I promised myself I'd explore the possibilities of obtaining a fur-buying license.

Tracks in the Mud

A trapping business was much like any other sole-proprietorship. I pretty much needed to be there every day. There were no times off for trappers during the fur season. Any days off were days without income. It was a seven-days-a-week deal. The traps had to be checked every day. Most days this was fine because I liked what I was doing and met each day with enthusiasm.

I remember one day when I began to feel pretty ill and had to stop to vomit several times. I don't know how I caught the stomach flu, but it hit me really hard. I stopped to talk to a landowner at mid-day, and as we talked I had to step around to the other side of the truck to be sick. He told me I should go home and go to bed. I finally made it home, and I remember it was a Friday. I was sick all night but woke up knowing I still had to check the traps. My wife, bless her heart, volunteered to drive since it was a Saturday. During the morning she had to stop numerous times to let me get out to be sick. Somehow we got the job done. Finally by evening I began to feel a bit better.

I remember a few other times when I was obviously running a high fever, but kept on plugging along and got the day done. There were hardships on the trap line, like blizzards and heavy rain or extreme cold. Sometimes the competition was tough, or muddy roads slowing my progress, but the worst was being sick. When that happened it really made the regular days seem great. One learned to count the blessings of a healthy day on the trap line.

For me the season was great. Fur prices were at historic levels and showed no sign of reversing. Muskrats were at the six-dollar level and raccoon were in the forty-dollar range. Coyotes were also in the forty- to fifty-dollar average price range. All furs were good. Long hair or short hair, it didn't seem to matter. Every time we sold fur, it seemed furs were firmer in price. I felt I couldn't go wrong investing in fur to re-sell. I also realized that people were spending more money on traps and equipment. Not only did I look into getting a fur buyer's license, but we also thought there was some potential in selling some supplies for trappers. All signs pointed to good demand for another season. Certainly we knew that the market would change eventually, but making hay when the sun shined was always a good thing.

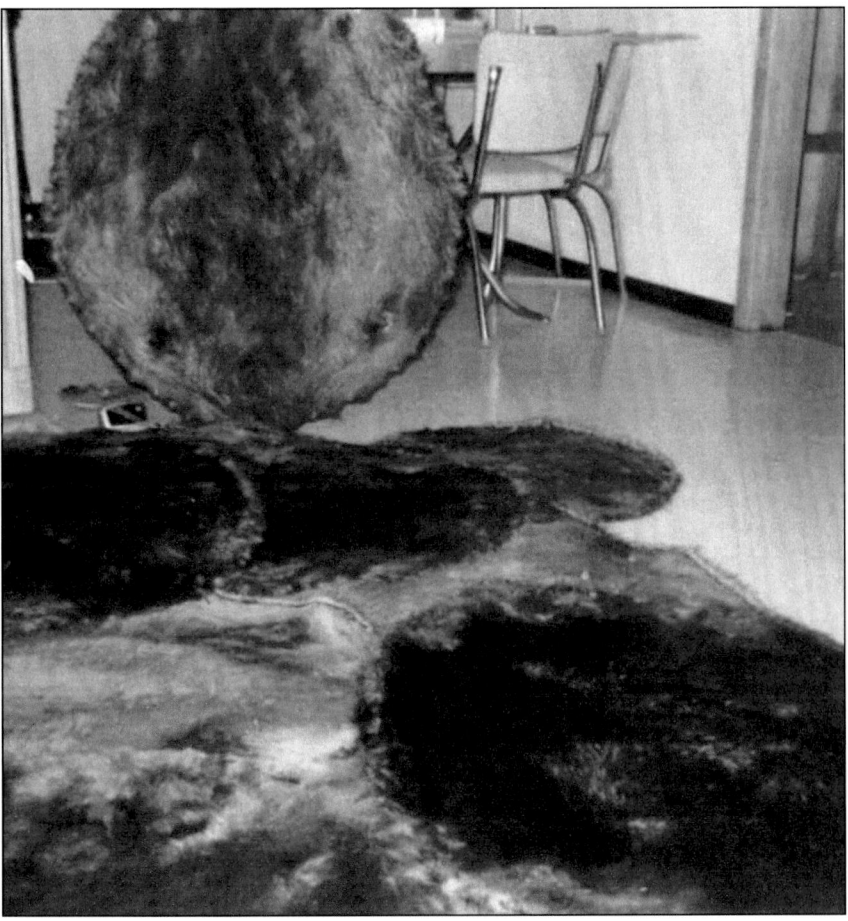

Beaver pelts, brushed and ready to ship to market.

Chapter 18

"Wheeling and Dealing, Grading and Trading"

WE WERE ALL PILED INTO THE TRUCK and the back of the truck was full. Our whole little family was ready to roll. I remember the wooden boxes stacked two-high and each one filled with un-stretched but dry 'coon pelts. "In the grease" we called them, or "green pelts" was the terminology. Other boxes held stretched and dried muskrat furs, packed one hundred to a box. On top of the stack of boxes were piled the stretched, fur-side-out coyote furs. Each one had been brushed and cleaned, and the fur glistened shiny and pale. We, of course had the sense to cover the whole pile of furs with blankets and lock the back of the truck topper, a prudent precaution with such a valuable load.

We started out well before dawn. The drive would be several hours at least. We had a few buyers in mind to give us bids on the furs. The first ones were just to keep the others honest. We'd figured and refigured the value of the various pelts and knew what they should be worth. Already we had a good idea who would buy the fur, but a couple of extra bids never hurt, to assure us we had gotten the best price.

We would stop for breakfast, and it would be a holiday of sorts. With my calculator in my pocket but the real calculator at my side, namely my wife, I was armed and ready to do battle with the fur graders.

It was a lot of work to carry in the whole load and have them all graded and then to repack the furs and go on for another bid, but we knew that after all the hard work of harvesting this crop the easiest thousands would be made by proper marketing.

The final stop was where we hoped to get the best bid. We knew this buyer well and reckoned he'd pick a "cotton" mink from the pile and throw it against the wall. We knew a few low grade "sow" 'coons would come out of the average, but we'd wrangle hard and play the earlier bids against this buyer. He wanted these furs, because he knew they were all well-handled and in good shape. These furs would help his average when he sold.

We got complemented on our nice coyotes, some of which were really nice "western" pale quality furs. He liked the color of our nice silver-toned racoons. Our mink were large, but of course he berated the brown color. Yet, we knew him to be the best mink buyer around. I also knew he would "nose-count" the muskrats and, despite the fact that some buyers offered me a higher price on the large sizes, the bottom line was better here because the average was much better.

We had kept all the numbers and all the offers, and in each category the totals were better than the other bids. Of course I got him to "round up" a bit more and throw in a new pair of shoulder-length trapping rubber gloves for free.

The deal was made and he cut us a check. The best part was that we knew his check was good. We had done business before and he was a reputable buyer. We left feeling we had gotten every dollar we could from our fur. Of course we put on a solemn face as we left. We would show no sign of happiness, no indication that we had gotten what we wanted. As we pulled out of the driveway of the buyer's place, we grinned at each other and exclaimed our joy at the prices. There would be supper on the way home, as well, the check tucked securely into my wife's purse, which never left her sight.

There was always some sadness as I sold the catch. A look into the empty back of the truck, where there had been the most beautiful soft pile of luxurious fur, now was only empty boxes. Such a fine, tangible pile of wealth traded for a piece of paper. If only we could afford to wear such rich clothes as those made from the beautiful renewable skins of the sleek furbearers. Our excited conversation went silent, and now as we drove, the sets re-played in my mind, the days wound back before my memory, of sunny, frosty mornings and gray, windy days. Each of them, I had come to know and not a catch was forgotten. The spirits of the furbearers of the past and their endless run to the horizon of time stayed with me. The silence, as the kids slept in the truck, was a reverence of the times and the places, a replay of the spinning tires and the silent streams. I paid tribute now to the shadows of the Sand Hills, the soft leaps along the stream banks, and the marauding bandits of the hollows and fence lines. I saw them all, and as they gave of their numbers for our family, I knew I too would give to keep their numbers strong, to preserve the habitat and help their ancestors to survive.

As we moved into another fur season, the expansion into some fur buying began to take shape. We now even had a separate checkbook that bore the name of our fur company. There was room on the stubs to itemize what was paid. The business was becoming more official, and we ran it like our other business. I found myself also building a new shed that summer. It was not large, but it would house my fur company. I had a place in time to equate myself with Jim Bridger or some other fur trader of times past. I had a space to connect myself to the fur booms of the past. The whole history of the settling of a continent condensed into my little fur shed. We felt we needed a place to buy fur, and store supplies. It was almost like having an office, really a pretty foreign concept for a trapper.

I began the process of obtaining a fur buyer's license. I went to the Game and Parks Commission in Lincoln and made application. There were rules for keeping exact records and obtaining trapping license numbers with each purchase. Selling records were also needed, and I even had to be bonded to be a fur buyer. All in all though, it was a fairly simple process at the time, to become a fur buyer. When I received my fur buyer's license, I felt I had taken a new step in the business world, and also a great leap into the fur boom. The plan was to hang out a shingle and buy some fur from the local folks who needed an outlet for their furs. There were lots of young trappers around and also the neighbors who shot a few coyotes on the way to town. We never intended buying to supersede the actual trapping, or to take time from it. We would be there by appointment and buy what furs we could.

Now the openness of the prairies was really beginning to grow on me. The winds that always blew in Nebraska each day brought their subtle stories: messages of the time of migration or harvest, drought or storm. The winds brought change to the way that our days were woven into our lives. So too, the winds of change moved the way that I looked at trapping and the fur industry as a whole.

The simple joy of being out there was still the best part of the experience, but the specter of legitimate occupation also became important. Trapping had gone from a pleasant avocation to a real paying job, and the idea of buying and selling fur added the possibility of more volume and more profit. The winds of change in the industry were sweeping regular folks like me to new levels of participation.

Traps and other equipment were now bought by the dozen or by the case. There were price breaks at various numbers of cases also. I now was buying everything wholesale and eying the possibility of re-selling trapping equipment to others. Of course much of the equipment was put to use on my own trap line.

The modification of traps was an exact science. Rarely were traps used just as they came from the box. Each trap was systematically put into a vise and strategically bent and adjusted. Pans were leveled, jaws were bent, and triggers were bent to the correct configuration. During this summer, all old traps were checked, repaired, and parts were replaced. I found where I could buy spare parts for all my traps and each and every trap was made like new. I was at a point where I wouldn't set anything but what I considered a perfectly functional and tuned trap. Any miss or malfunction would quite likely mean the loss of a forty-five dollar 'coon or other equally valuable furbearer. With the competition, I might never get another chance at that catch. Perfectly tuned and functioning traps also meant solid, humane catches, and, therefore, the best outcome for the resource in general.

Culling, repairing, and replacing equipment took many summer days. This time was filled with memories and also with anticipation as the trap line, past and future, played across my mind. The pleasant thoughts, as my hands worked on and caressed the steel made this time almost sacred and certainly not unpleasant. Numbers were tallied and recorded and all equipment was totaled. Locations for sets were solid in my mind, and I knew what would be needed to quickly and efficiently cover my trap line and harvest the crop. I had reached the point where I bought long rubber gloves and hip boots, not by the pair, but by the several pair, always having an extra pair if one got snagged on a barbed-wire fence or a protruding beaver cutting.

It seems there was always a season or event that marked the year. For many it was their birthday or possibly their wedding anniversary. Fishing season opener marked the year for a lot of people. For me the pivotal point of the year was the turning of the leaves, the reddening of the milo crop and the first scraping of the windshield of frost.

Those of us who spend a lot of time outdoors, I believed, were more in tune with the length of the days. I marked the sun as it set and rose, where it was on the horizon and the shortening of the days as well as the sun's migration to more southerly starts and stops. These signs triggered the urge to be in the field. Maybe I realized that ticks and mosquitoes were waning, or maybe it was the old instinct to pursue the winter's provisions, by hunting, but at any rate a quickness of step and clarity of purpose seemed to fill us in the fall.

With a toddler and a baby, we again cruised the back-roads. Our buying business was doing all right and so I approached the trapping season with confidence and less pressure to produce. Organization of the trapping was pretty good now, and I had a positive feeling about what could be accomplished.

There would be no split in the opening of the trapping seasons this year. The whole state would open at the same time. I did, however, elect to run a trap line into the area I had trapped during the early season the previous year. The research was complete, and I felt I could handle the area in addition to my regular areas. The fur sign was good in that area, and I felt I couldn't pass up the extra fur. The state lakes were still a "free-for-all" situation, so I would have to compete on all the public areas.

Tracks in the Mud

School began and I remained busy with other work into the fall. Fortunately most of my fur prospecting and landowner relations had been completed. As the evenings cooled, there was time to travel to the reservoirs and watch the muskrats swim as they prepared for winter and enjoyed the last days of the sunlight and free air, before their entrapment under the ice of winter.

As the season opened, I really felt I had to get an accurate handle on the market. All indications were that it would be good. I called my buyers and discussed pricing, since I would be attempting to buy some fur this season. People called me to find out what I'd pay, and I in turn checked out what the local buyers were paying. Some of them also called me or had a trapper friend call to see what I was paying.

The country market for fur was highly speculative. Buyers want to buy fur or they won't make any money, yet they certainly don't want to pay more than they should. The market was established by what the local rural buyers paid. We were in a time when most people felt that if one was paying a certain price it must be okay. "If he can do it, so can I," was the prevailing attitude. We decided from the beginning we would not over-pay. We didn't have a lot of money to invest, and of course our biggest investment was in the actual trapping operation.

My thought was to buy mostly unskinned fur and try to make my money with a little sweat: skinning and finishing the fur and maybe waiting to see if the market advanced. I felt I could do pretty well at grading the fur and felt my buyers would treat me fairly.

As it turned out it was one of the best years ever to begin fur buying. It was almost a "no-brainer." The demand for fur was reaching its peak, and all fur—even low grades—were easy to sell in the worldwide market.

Fortunately any mistakes I made were covered by a rising market and the fact that we had some pretty good outlets for our fur. Late in the season, when the snow came and people began shooting coyotes with high-power rifles, most buyers were paying about twenty dollars for shot, in-carcass coyotes. We felt there was pretty good money to be made since the stretched and finished coyotes were worth fifty dollars in our market. Fortunately, I had become pretty good with a needle and thread after many years of fox and coyote hunting and I could sew up bullet holes in coyote skins and then brush out the blood after the fur was turned fur side out. The finished product was very nice and commanded top dollar on the market. During the time of year before the coyotes began to rub they were petty easy to buy without making any mistakes. My wife bought carcass coyotes and had never stopped reminding me of how good she was at it. She'd pay twenty dollars and say "put it over there." I had to skin the critter and sew it up, but we doubled our money.

My wife's favorite memory concerning fur buying was her venture into the skunk-fur market. I was out trapping and some guys stopped in with some fur to sell. They had a whole garbage sack full of skunk skins. They hadn't found anyone to buy them I guess, but my wife remembered that one of our buyers bought a lot of skunk skins and had a good market for them. She offered them two dollars each and asked how many they had. They were happy to get them sold and even told her the correct number. She never counted them and threw them into the freezer in a double bag. We thawed them out and dumped them on our buyer's floor. He counted them and paid us five dollars each. My wife always remarked what a profitable item skunk fur can be.

The guy who bought those skunks told me he eventually ended up buying most of the skunks in the U.S. He apparently had a good market for them in Italy at the time. After telling me about all the skunks he bought and sold, he remarked that, "It's a tough way to serve the Lord." My only comment to my wife was that if she started buying them in the carcass, I was going to draw the line.

The fur buying was really a very insignificant part of our fur business, but it was very interesting and really broadened the experience of the fur-boom days. Trapping was still the real bread-and-butter part of our fall and winter.

Boom era "soft gold" ready for market.

Chapter 19

"Wild Trails"

I SUPPOSE ALL TRAPPERS HAVE STORIES of some really great catches, and I remember one such occasion during that season. I had a stretch of creek-bottom I had obtained permission to trap. It required a half-mile walk through some pretty dense brush and rugged terrain to reach. I saved the spot for later in the season because it would take some time to trap. I decided to carry in five 220 Conibear traps to the spot. I got into the deep creek and found a fifty-yard stretch where numerous 'coon trails crossed and recrossed the creek and the sign of their working the banks for crayfish was unbelievable. I dug in five pocket sets with Conibears in this small stretch of stream. Upon my return to the locations, I found five dead racoons in the five Conibears. I reset the traps and loaded two 'coons into my pack-basket, piled one on top of the basket and carried one in each hand for the trek out to the truck. As I struggled through the heavy brush and up and down the ravines, I slipped and slid into some brush. A sharp stick jammed right into my ear, and I found myself with blood spurting out of my ear. I stopped it the best

I could and somehow made it out to my truck. I got the bleeding stopped but seemed to have very little hearing in that ear. I headed home and decided I had better have a doctor have a look at the ear. After cleaning it out, he said I had slightly perforated the eardrum, but said it should be all right. It hurt like the dickens but healed up. The next trip to the creek bottom yielded another five racoons from those five sets. The third trip netted two more, and I decided to pull the sets and count my blessings.

So it was again the time of year when I became them, when I entered their lives and walked in their tracks. At that time of year, I was the muskrat as I half swam and half walked in the syrupy mire. I followed my cut channels through silt and the roots of aquatic vegetation. I picked my way through tunnels that led to bank dens, keeping close to the bottom of the runs. I approached the mats of vegetation, placing one front foot then the other upon the water-soaked perimeter of the feed bed. I pushed with my back feet up on the floating mass of roots and stems. Moment by moment, I took a breath of the still night air and dove to dig roots and push vegetation upon the reed hummocks.

I was the raccoon running the bare ridges as the wind and ice pierce my heavy under-fur and drive me, eyes tearing in the sleet, to the warm spring-holes. My belly ached with the frozen grass, and I felt the earth's life blood as I entered the water. The wind was barred from harassing me, and I felt the squirming food in the crayfish holes and crunched the succulent frogs. Here the water flowed from the heart of life and gave respite from the impending winter. Soon, even this respite would not be enough. Now I gorged on the foods of fat. The water buoyed me up, and I went eye-level to the waterline and sought the banks that yielded food. I worked by feeling and touching each hole and depression. Half floating and half walking I searched the slick mud. Following the paths of my brothers, I was led to the modest days of hibernation. Soon I parted the reeds and slid beneath the low branches of the willows and followed my senses to the comfort of a den.

Sometimes I was the coyote, condemned to run those frozen hills, no days of hibernation to call me home. I was hardened now, as I had seen the dirt-hole sets of the trappers and I had dived to safety as bullets and hounds sought my tight hide. The moon moved me to hunt the edges of the waterways and caused all life to shun my presence. The gnawing was endless now and temptation was everywhere, to feed and be satisfied. I kept to the section lines and brush coulees. Rodents were my life, and last fall's rotting offal was my desert. I was driven by constant hunger and constant fear. Yet my senses were honed and I would pass the winter and then be invincible. I would walk in my own tracks and pass the same safe crossings, going under fences and keeping to my old trails.

I was in their heads and in their skins. I ran the stream banks and poked my head into every hole and crevice. My slick, shiny fur bristled as I entered and left the water of the stream. I was the mink and I ripped the flesh from tiny rodents and aquatic life. Muskrats were my prize, and I explored their dens and followed their trails under the frozen ponds. I could breathe their air and invade their dens. I was the spring-coiled lithe predator of the waterways.

Beyond the quarry whose tracks I followed and duplicated, above the paths I followed and the roots that I dug, and past all the deep warm pools in the streams that I swam and traversed, I was the coyote. I was the wolf, the alpha predator. I was the lone ghost that traversed the dusty cow trails. I was the wisp of smoke that slipped across the sun-soaked ridge. Only the lonely, hungry predator could squeeze the life-blood from the land. I was the hungry killer, seeking

Tracks in the Mud

to wrench subsistence from the sodden trails and ice-rimmed streams. Only the trapper who was hungry and wanting would rise to the level of competition to make the catches that passified the pack.

My goals and needs were those of the predator. We needed the fur check and only the predator stayed out, hunted the storms and never gave up. Only the predator took to the trails of the prey, knowing the hiding places of the quarry, and followed to the end of each trail. The human predator learned from the coyote and overtook even the master of the wild.

Now I had truly stepped beyond the boundaries of reality. I had gone where I had never thought I could travel. I lived the life of the trapper and made a living at it. I was the wolfer, the mountain man, the trader. Each morning the frozen air hit my face well before the sun, the cold tightened my skin and the season cut into my nostrils. I smelled the air of the frozen landscape and it breathed excitement into my being.

Each day I dug the keys from my pocket, checked with the light beam to see that all the simple tools were in place: the bucket of bait, the digging tool, the wire and pliers, the cable-cutters, and the handgun. I knew the reason for the coyote's howl, the addiction to the full moon, the sense of knowing the reason that I ran the lonely trails.

The tires groaned and ran flat-sided on the cold pavement, the transmission of the truck was stiff and the gears caught only with great reluctance and pain. We should not be driven so hard and long on such pensive days.

Coffee steamed the windshield, the wiper-blades clawed at the fresh scrapings of ice on the glass, and frozen weeds danced along the roadside. The beauty of such black-and-white days sharpened the senses. The eyes of a deer in the headlights pierced the blackness and turned to leave the roadway. The wild always gave us premonitions and mapped out the tortuous paths we must follow.

This was the mellow time, the drive during which the truck heater took the sharpness from my bones and lulled my mind to contemplation. The day was still perfection, and the sets played in my mind. Of course, my mind gave me hope of all things clicking perfectly. The new sets in the saddle on the ridge at the Kubic place had all connected. The big buck mink that frequented the spring-hole set by Denton had worked my new set arrangement and was held waiting for my check. The colony traps in the new marsh were filled to capacity, and the raccoons had worked the deep creeks during the cold, windy night.

Today my mind created the perfect storm, the flawless run, the big day to make my week one of the best. Yet, the day would play as it had been planned by the movements in the night. There was a coyote, but not in the new saddle, instead a snare in a fence crossing had connected. A racoon invaded an old barn I had set and met the frozen jaws of a Connibear. The muskrats came in singles as I checked pocket sets in moving water areas, yet unfrozen, and Conibears in dens at a lake. There was the surprise beaver in a narrow creek run. The fur boxes in the truck looked like wages would be earned, but no windfall profits.

The biggest event of the day would occur as I traveled home on a dark tar road. Cruising along at fifty-five miles an hour, I rounded a curve with a steep embankment. From somewhere below my line of sight, a big white-tailed buck jumped from below the ditch and landed right in the front end of my pickup. Momentarily it seemed like the end of the world as he hit the radiator and also put out both headlights, sending the hood up. The world went black, and when I stopped, the deer was dead and so was my truck. The fan was crushed into the radiator.

Tracks in the Mud

I walked to a nearby farm and got a ride home. I was able to get someone to tow the truck in to be fixed, and I worked out an arrangement with my wife to use her car to check traps the next morning while my truck was being fixed.

The day played out somewhat differently than my mind had conjectured in the morning, but that was some of the beauty of the trap line. No days were ever completely planned, and one pretty much needed to let go and follow the flow. The trap line taught one to be flexible and to give in to what would be. I suspected that even the most mind-numbed, routine-oriented robot would be transformed by a season on the trap line. There might be a good plan for the season, but each day led to its own conclusion, each trap checked points to the next logical move, and each day and each change in the weather dictated the next logical step to getting the harvest completed. Often the tail wagged the dog. The weather changed and our days were changed.

I heard it before I woke up. It was announcing itself on our window. The tapping soon seeped into my consciousness, and as I awakened I knew the day would bring its own brand of excitement. The weather had been cold, but now seemed to have softened, as it so often did in Nebraska during the winter. What I heard on the windows seemed less hard than what I would have guessed at that time of year. Sure enough, it was rain, totally liquid, that announced the day. My day would be changed from what I had thought it would be. Dirt sets would now be rendered useless. There would be water running over the ice on streams. The snow on lakes would be gone giving me another chance of finding muskrat and beaver dens. Every weather change brought both hardship and opportunity.

The skies were still spitting a few drops of water as I got into the truck. The day was not yet settled upon what it would be but the beginning of a wind change to the northwest told me a change was on the agenda. A change in the weather was no surprise in Nebraska. I knew a lot of walking was in my future as the dirt roads would be impassable and there would be no driving on farmers' field roads after the rain.

My first area to check was a stream, and as I went down to the water's edge I stuck my ice chisel into the ice beneath a running stream of last night's rain. Not only would the icy walk be treacherous and slippery, but downright dangerous. I would not like even to conjecture upon the consequences of falling through weakened ice in these conditions. Slipping along the half-frozen banks, I made it to the open patches of spring-fed water where sets had been made. The good news of the winter thaw was the amount of fur movement during the warm spell. The water line produced well and the mixed bag of winter trapping was well represented by muskrats, a mink, and a raccoon.

I proceeded to a marsh where the now-snow-free ice opened up the possibility of new sets under the clear frozen layer. I also packed dry dirt into some coyote sets and prepared them for the inevitable re-freeze of the next nights. Fire and ice made and broke the trapper. More and more I learned about change and flexibility. I learned to plan and forge ahead and then give in to the conditions that prevailed.

Chapter 20
"New Red Fords and Barred Windows"

STILL I SEE THE OLD TRUCKS, the rusted fenders, the headlamps burned out and the doors wired shut. Old sedans with trunks lifted at bridge crossings where the water met the road, parked at the roadside as mud-splattered teenagers tended traps after school. There were the old coats kept shut with safety pins and the tattered caps with ear-flaps pulled down. These things have always been the trapper's meager stock in trade. Yet the prosperity had brought a new element to the trap line.

As I ran into other trappers that fur-boom year, I thought back to the movie *Jeremiah Johnson* in which Robert Redford starred as the title character. Johnson ran into an old grizzly hunter far back in the mountains after several seasons living the life of a mountain man. After sharing a couple of bites of something broiled on a stick over an open fire, the old grizzly hunter commented, "You've come far, Pilgrim." So I looked at trappers as a group and realized that we too had come far.

As I drove over a hill the next creek crossing came into sight. There was a steel bridge. My notes said there was lots of 'coon sign under the bridge. The bad news was that there was a truck parked there. As I got close, I could see it was a shiny red Ford four-by-four. It was a very new rig with a matching fiberglass topper with shiny chrome strips along its sides—not the rig most trappers drove.

I stopped and got out of my truck and gave a quick glance inside the back of the parked truck. Newly-dyed black coil springs with perfectly cut chains lay in neat piles in the back of the truck. The stakes were all identical, and the bait buckets were neatly stored. There was lots of equipment, and it appeared this guy was pretty serious about trapping 'coon.

I peered over the railing and muddy water flowed from beneath the bridge. I could see two neatly constructed pocket sets. As I turned, a camouflage hat appeared, coming up the bank. The name of some sporting goods company was printed on the front of the cap.

"How you doing?" I opened as he found footing on the road.

"Okay," he returned. His waders were squeaky-new, and he wore a perfectly matched set of rubber gloves.

"Trapping 'coon?"

"Yeah."

"Lotta sign on this bridge."

"Should be a good season."

He proceeded to tell me he was from Omaha, and was running a long 'coon line. He'd quit his construction job, taken trapping instructions from a big-name trapping instructor out west and was going to trap all season. He hadn't grown up trapping but really had the urge to be a trapper, to experience the freedom and adventure of the full-time trap line.

"I'm going to trap 'coon in Nebraska for a few weeks, then head to Colorado for a while and work on beaver, 'rats, and 'coon. Then I'll head down to Arizona and trap coyotes and bobcats."

Tracks in the Mud

He had taken the whole package of instruction and used his savings to buy a pretty nice outfit. "Foreigner" was rocking on his tape player as he hopped into the truck and sped to his next location.

I crossed paths with him at a few more streams, where his trap line and mine randomly crossed. He set each location the same and although his "cookie cutter" approach was surely efficient, it was also easy to trap around and "downstream" of him. He made some catches to be certain and his 'coon were held well and humanely. With enough traps in the water he should have done okay. The prices were good, and he seemed like a hard worker. Soon, though, "Mr. Red Ford" had moved on, and there was still plenty of fur left.

Now I met other trappers in the fall as the trapping season began. They drove brand new four-wheel drive pickups. They had custom license plates like "FUR GTR" or "RATMAN." The era of the "long-liner" the "state-hopper" had arrived. These were the guys who could afford to take vacations from work and trap big time. Some were professionals who worked at it full time. These "new era" pros were not "boot-strapping" it. They had invested in the best equipment and vehicles. Change had come, brought on by high prices and the in-born desire for the freedom and fulfillment of a lifestyle that was thought to be obsolete for so long.

"Mr. New Ford" was precise, punctuated, trained and efficient. Although he had trapped a bit as a kid, he really came into the sport as a result of good instruction and the sincere craving for the freedom of the trap line. He paid his tuition instead of paying his dues like a lot of us. I suppose there was a bit of resentment for someone who bought the knowledge that some of us spent long hard years to develop.

Now it was almost an entitlement; we expected high prices. We also anticipated high competition on the trap line. The whole game was ramped-up, escalated to a new level of business. People were ready to pay anything to get training in fur harvesting. No trap was too expensive if it did the job well. No lure was ruled out if it helped to bring in the quarry. Trapping was big business, big interstate business. One day the competition was crawling up your stream bank, the next they were in New Mexico. The good news was that after a couple of harsh cold fronts in Nebraska, the next warm spell was mine. I cherished the winter days when I saw no other trappers or any sign of them. The fair-weather guys left, and the thaws of January were all mine.

The peak of the fur boom had arrived. The signs were there. Optimism pervaded the whole industry from trappers to buyers to the ultimate consumer. It seemed it could go on forever, yet most knew deep down it couldn't last. High prices on raw fur were the most obvious indication of the boom. Definitely prices were good. It didn't matter what was targeted, it was probably worthwhile. Even the lowly 'possum paid the gas bills. I remember a cartoon in a trapping magazine a few years later as the fur prices were beginning to cool down. It showed a set location where someone had obviously stolen a fox or coyote out of someone else's set but in one trap there was an opossum. The caption read: "Prices must be down. They're leaving the grinners."

Now long hair was moving as well as short hair. Mixed water lines paid well and the dry-land game was equally prosperous. There was no need for boredom with trapping of one or two species.

Beyond the price of fur, the signs of the boom peaking were everywhere. Indeed people were wearing fur, which was really the bottom line driving force behind the whole phenomenon. My wife always said that a red fox coat would really be nice. Despite the fact that we trapped foxes, we still couldn't justify having them made into a coat when the raw price was so high. "When they come down in price" we decided.

With so many trappers in the field, there were also the unfortunate mishaps of pets being captured accidentally by some of the many inexperienced trappers out there. The trapping organization quickly implemented training requirements for new trappers and really took a proactive role in keeping the fur harvesters doing a good job. Yet much damage was done to the image of the trapper by out-of-proportion media coverage of some unfortunate incidents. Actually the mishaps were amazingly few when one considered the millions of traps set in the U.S. during these years. I was sure many more dogs got hit by cars during those years than were accidentally caught in a fox set.

Beyond the fairly regular thefts of fur from traps, I guess the real intensity of the fur business hit home for me, at our home. It was November of 1980. My guess was that the late seventies were some of the best years in that almost all fur was valuable. Some items may have peaked during other years but the late seventies for me were the best with most common items such as muskrat, raccoon, mink, coyote, fox, and beaver all being profitable. By 1980 the value of fur was well known. Fur buyers were being targeted by thieves who knew there was a ready market for fur. Since most fur items had no special way to identify them, thieves could just take the fur to another buyer in a different area and sell them. The early market that year was strong, and most trappers and fur buyers felt it would be a great year. Indeed it was still a great year and both trapping and fur buying were going well.

For us it was a special November also, because our third daughter was born during that month. I made it to the delivery room for the birth and all went well. It was indeed a very busy time and

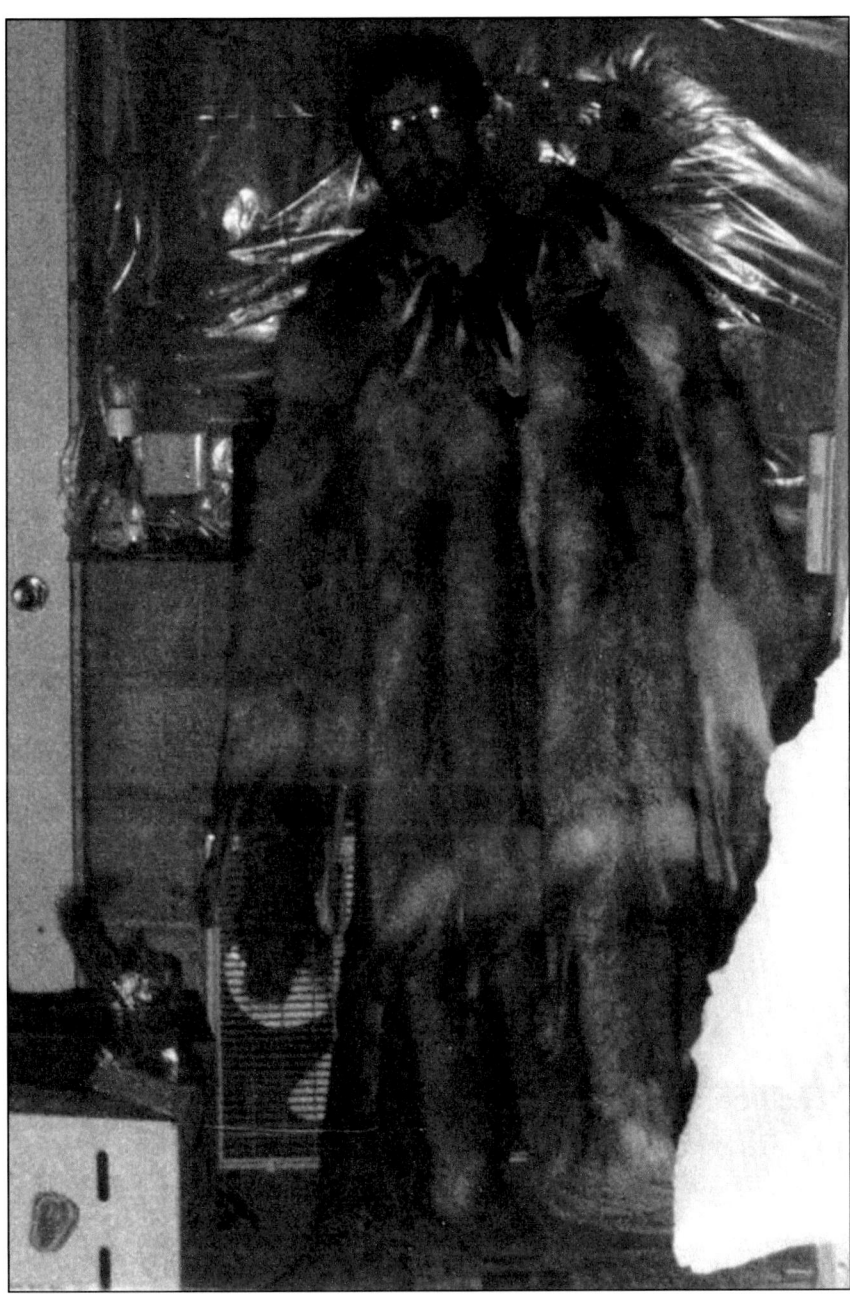
Top quality fox pelts.

Tracks in the Mud

yet all the traps got run and life went on. It was a very positive month and, to a trapper, November was the best month, probably the one that set the stage for all the other months. Yet this November the real craziness of the fur boom hit me hard.

We had that little shed where we bought fur and processed some fur as well. I suppose as a small country fur dealer, I was a bit vulnerable. We had no security system except a big padlock on the shed. Fortunately I never kept any fur in the shed overnight. It was all moved to another location. When I found the lock pried off the door one morning and the shed ransacked, I was happy I had taken the precaution of storing fur elsewhere. Of course we reported the break-in to the local authorities but nothing ever came of it. When one lived in rural Nebraska and hardly thought of locking doors it was a real shocker to get broken into. I guess in those years hanging out a sign that said "fur buyer" was an invitation to would-be thieves. It was an eerie feeling to know that someone broke into my building and meant to steal from me. I guess it was no worse than someone lifting a mink from my set, but the invasion of one's property was very unnerving. I guess I never felt that breaking and entering to steal fur would ever be a possibility. Money drove a lot of activity, both good and bad.

The prime season that year was good, and prices remained strong. The weather was tolerable and fur numbers were good. My memory now settles upon the later part of the season. The early uncertainty of price and demand in the marketplace was past. We had stopped, gotten bids, and sold our early season and most of our main season fur. The prices had been good and now, with our last lot of the season, we pretty much knew what the various items would bring, and to whom we would sell them. We were headed to a longtime buyer who we had done business with for many years. Some of my earliest fur sales were here, and we knew what he would pay and how the sale would conclude. Certainly we had graded and re-graded, we had multiplied the numbers and knew what we must get. We also knew that this buyer knew our fur and also knew what he must pay to buy our fur.

This would be a low-stress trip. We might buy a few supplies for the trap line and would enjoy the day. We arrived at Oberlund Hide and Fur/Northern Trapline Supply at ten in the morning. It was still a busy place but not the utter zoo of November and December. The buying building was still the original metal shed. As I entered, the smell of fox urine and skunk essence mingled with 'coon fat greeted my nostrils. Really a pretty agreeable smell, bringing back instant memories of the early fall trap line. Yes, I suppose it smelled like money, yet these were the smells that compared to the country smell of freshly cut alfalfa or the smell after a rainstorm, or I suppose even the smell of wood smoke on a cold winter's night. Smells brought back memories and visions of times past or times anticipated more than anything else.

The visuals also greeted us as I saw boxes of new traps along the wall and even a glass case with high-quality skinning knives and rifle scopes. On the wall was a huge bear trap with jaws clamped open and a price tag of $150.00—"great conversation piece." A number one long-spring trap on the wall had its pan painted red with a sign that read, "Press the red button if you wish to complain about the service."

On the other wall there were wire fur stretchers of all sizes for sale. Bundles of stakes hung on the poles in the room and mounted furbearers adorned the counters and spaces on the wall where nothing was offered for sale.

The smells and displays were much the same as they had been twenty years earlier, but the place had changed a lot since the

Author and son with mink, coyote, and fox pelts.

up-swing in the fur market. Several new out buildings had sprung up, used for warehousing trapping supplies, for skinning, and processing the large volume of fur now being produced. There were also new security systems and bars across the windows. Oh, how times had changed.

There were now separate rooms for grading and buying fur, offering privacy and a more relaxed atmosphere for the haggling over fur prices. The owner had other people who helped buy, but I knew we would deal directly with the owner. He was not a man of easy smiles or courteous pleasantries, yet today he actually greeted me with a slight smile and a comment about the weather. Apparently he had sold some fur and perhaps the stress of the season was waning for him as well. He had a cold chunk of a cigar clamped in the corner of his mouth. He seemed to chew on it all day, but I don't ever remember him having it lit. His gruff demeanor definitely turned some people away, but I always felt it was a purposeful wall to keep chiselers at bay. Photos on the wall showed him with fur caught on the trap line. He of course knew first hand the work trappers put into their catch, yet he had to buy and sell at a profit. He had risen from the ranks of hip-boot-clad bush-whackers just as most fur buyers seemed to have done.

The buying room had a long counter along the wall—plenty of room to spread large volumes of fur to be graded. The blue paint had been long worn from most of the wooden counter from thousands of skins being graded and removed from the counter.

Our furs were all organized in wooden crates, and as we brought them in, we set the crates next to the bench. We knew our fur buyer would dump the boxes out on the counter and any pre-arrangement of the grades would be disrupted by his random dump of the boxes.

Tracks in the Mud

"So what do you think these 'rats are worth?" he toyed with me.

"You'll have to look at them," I countered.

"You know the Asian market is a little soft on 'rats now."

"I heard the Europeans are buying them as fast as they can get ahold of 'em."

He grunted and turned a few of the furs inside out, inspected the pelts, and blew into the fur.

"I'll tell you what I can do here. I'll nose count these 'rats at six-seventy-five. I won't throw out any kits, we'll just count 'em out at six-seventy-five."

"You won't find any kits in this lot. I think it's a seven-twenty-five market today, and you know it's a very clean and damage-free bunch of 'rats."

He rustled around in the pile of muskrat hides a bit, hemmed and hawed at me. "Okay just for old time's sake, I'll go seven dollars nose count on them, but I'll probably lose the farm over it." And so we agreed on a price.

The 'coons and coyotes were next to be graded and finally some miscellaneous mink, beaver, fox, and badger were haggled over.

My wife did the final check on the numbers. As she calculated it all, the buyer as usual offered her a job because of her incredible math skills. She politely declined, and we all had a good laugh.

As he cut the check, "Anything you want to deduct in the way of traps or supplies?"

"What kind of a dozen-price can you give me on the 220 Conibears?"

He scraped through a pile of price sheets and finally came up with a price. I offered him five dollars per dozen less than he asked and his response was, "Well I'm losing the farm anyway, I might as well go in a little deeper."

So we bought some traps and sold some fur. We were happy and I'm sure he came out just fine on his end.

The most basic form of capitalism had just occurred. A method of trade and price-point adjustment had played out in the oldest, most basic level. It was some of the greatest business I had ever conducted. Traders and trappers all across this land had practiced the same form of business for centuries. I liked to think our great economic system was spawned on this same great tradition of the fur trade.

The ride home from marketing fur was always one of mixed emotions. We were happy to have turned a lot of hard work into cash, yet there was always the sense of loss when the beautiful fur has been turned in for a piece of paper. We had pictures of the catch and that helped, but there was always a sense of sadness as a fur season ended. Soon I could begin anew and start scouting for fur sign. The cycle of the trapper's life much paralleled the cycle of nature.

Chapter 21

"Tracks North"

UNKNOWN TO ME I HAD JUST COMPLETED my second to the last season of tapping in Nebraska. The winds of change were blowing. My wife was offered a teaching job in Minnesota in the hometown where I had grown up. It was an opportunity to move near my relatives and ultimately an opportunity for our kids to be near their grandparents. We decided to make the move and struggled with the sale of our place and how I could move my other business to Minnesota. I still had a lot of trapping territory and I knew there was income potential there in the fall.

As it turned out, our place didn't sell until late summer and didn't close until late fall. My wife had to make the move to Minnesota, and I would stay to finish our sale and also to trap one more season before the move to Minnesota.

Although the season of 1980 had finished strong, there were signs that the markets were beginning to soften. I knew I didn't want to invest in the buying of fur when prices seemed to be falling. I was confident I could make some money by trapping my territory and selling the fur, but the risk of buying was out of the question.

Fortunately the move was mostly completed in the summer, as we knew we had to move and must sell our house. I returned to Nebraska to a virtually bare house to hit the trapping season. If ever there was a season of pure profit-taking this was it. The plan was to take as much easy fur as possible before the weather turned miserable and then hopefully to close on the house and move north. From a trapping standpoint, it was in reverse of what most trappers did, but I had much to do in Minnesota to be able to hit the ground running at my other business when spring came. We were fortunate enough to be able to buy some land and build a house in Minnesota, so I was back and forth a few times to help get that done.

The names and the faces of landowners still dance in my mind. The tree-edged draws, the rolling pastureland and the deep slippery creek bottoms all meld together as I remember. The Salt Creek drainage, the Little Blue valley, the Nemaha, and the countless streams and stock ponds still are etched into the program of my memory. Geography is such an intimate and detailed thing to a trapper. We don't just see blue lines on maps. We see where those lines cross roads and we visualize bridges and steep muddy banks under those bridges. We see the curve in a stream where a 'coon track-lined trail crossed a sand bar downstream from the bridge. The places where the spring holes stayed open all winter and the mink and 'coon fed on the abundant crayfish in those locations still draw my attention on a map of the area. I remember how the water flowed and how it drained the state. Every deep cut across a pasture brought memories of coyotes and the mental smell of sweet lures and acrid squirts of urine on a set. Now as I write these words some thirty years later I can still see the dirt roads, and can retrace those old trap lines across those windswept counties.

Nebraska was a hard place to come to and now a hard place to contemplate leaving. Although I had cut my trapping teeth in

Tracks in the Mud

Minnesota, I ripped into the meat and potatoes of it in Nebraska, as the fur market matured and my abilities grew. The last season here would be cut short. I would only trap the prime early part of the season. The idea was to give it all I could, take all the fur possible in a short time and then head to Minnesota. I had other commitments there that also needed to be addressed.

This was the season that the handwriting was really on the wall as fur prices began to drop. As I recall, the early sales in the country were pretty high as speculation was still high. As demand proved to be down, many buyers lost money and the whole market came down. I was happy I wasn't buying any fur and also happy I had sold furs fairly early as the market did not seem to advance later in the season.

It was still November when I made those final checks and pulled stakes from tough mud and solid soil. A few last golden sunsets laid shadows across deep creeks as I hip-booted my way among sand bars and tall grass banks. I found that it really wasn't the great fur resource or the excellent trapping territory I was leaving behind, but the memories that lurked behind every stock dam and the folks who lived and sometimes struggled behind the lighted windows of farmhouses strung across the rolling prairie. Most interesting to me was how the Nebraska countryside grew on me and made me feel at home. It was a place that changed a trapper and probably for the better. I had come here with the idea that lakes and marshes and forested areas were the trapper's paradise I had dreamed of, and now I knew that paradise could take many forms.

Still I heard the coyotes sing and knew of their perpetuity, knew they would outlast me on these merciless plains. I followed the fresh tracks of raccoon on familiar streams and realized they would survive my season here. The land and the fur went on and remained commingled in their mutual wildness. I would pull up my wildness as I struggled to remove the rebar stakes from the prairie soil and travel it to other places. The shadows of the Nebraska landscape would always haunt my memory. I stopped to wonder who would next travel these streams, pound steel into the banks, and puzzle out the trails and how they should be best set for the fur that ran them. I wondered who would next talk to the farmers to get permission, if my name would come up in the trapping conversation, and if indeed permissions would again be granted to some anxious trapper. Some of my locations would surely be set by someone else, the descendents of these furbearers would fill other folks' fur stretchers, and those same golden sunsets would fall upon the shoulders of other fur-seekers.

    I wondered too, who my predecessors might have been. Perhaps they were mountain men who got stuck on the plains and found the streams ready for their trap lines. Surely Native Americans plodded these same waterways carrying snares and building deadfalls to take the fur. Settlers found extra income from these same waterways and hills. Other residents upon the land found the necessity to control the coyotes that threatened their enterprises. Motives can change but the wildlife maintains continuity and happily we can merge with it in our time.

    It seems as though home wasn't always where we thought it was. Just as the thousands of acres I had made my own, reached for my heart, and as the final traps were pulled from Nebraska soil, I knew that the trail ahead was always the most interesting. Coming back to trap was the best way to say good-bye to the land I had been tied to for so many years. We parted on good terms, and now I left and the land was as if I had not been upon it. I think that was the way it was with trappers. We have always believed that the land

Tracks in the Mud

should be left as we found it. Even the mountain men of years gone by never had an enormous impact upon the land. Now I looked at the trail ahead. We had built a new house in Minnesota and family made it a home. So now I headed back to Minnesota with my last load of belongings. It consisted of mostly trapping and outdoor gear, along with a nice bunch of fur. I had lived with no furniture in the house since all our other things had been moved. I ate on an old table and slept in my sleeping bag on the floor. By cramming everything I could possibly put into the cab and packing the back topper of the truck, I had everything along.

It was great to be back in Minnesota. Our family was again together and of course we were now much closer to all of our families. There was much work to be done both on our house and also on our other business. My wife had a great teaching job, and I had work to do to hit the ground running with my work. We knew that trapping would play a less-important role in our lives and livelihood, but I still would trap to supplement our income and of course to continue to do what I enjoy.

The changes were probably harder to overcome than the lower fur prices. Many fine muskrat sloughs were now in the backyards of huge houses. The amount of trapping competition was fierce, since Minnesota had always been a state where trappers had been abundant. Yet I guessed I had learned a few things about competition, and it bothered me less now, less than it would have ten years earlier. The boom had brought with it a lot of trappers, but also a larger fraternity of people who appreciated the art.

Much had changed in my home area. Many of the places where I had trapped as a young trapper were now built up with homes. Many wild areas had been converted to residential developments. Of course the lakes and streams where I had cut my trapping teeth were now being trapped by others. Yet many of the landowners who had given permission to trap in earlier years were still there and remembered me and my brother. There would be places to trap. Prices on fur were beginning to slip. I remember that the fur I brought from Nebraska sold for maybe two thirds of what it had brought the previous season. The next season, prices were similar or a little lower.

Chapter 22

"Post-Boom Days"

For me it was a star-crossed foray into the sky-embraced prairie. Whatever it was that brought me to the plains of Nebraska during the greatest fur boom in modern history, it was a destiny beyond anything I could have planned. I suppose I would have scoffed at even the thought of moving to the Cornhusker State, yet there I was, and set to ride the wave of common-fur in one of the best places imaginable. Now, returned to Minnesota, after a flash in the pan, a run incomparable to anything imaginable to one who aspired for a shot at being a professional trapper, fur prices waned and other opportunities became available, I found myself in the place of my up-bringing.

By the next season they were already dropping like flies. The early eighties brought substantial drops in most fur prices, and trapper numbers also fell off considerably. For people like me and a good number of dedicated trappers, it was actually pretty welcome. There was a little more room and a few less trappers. The quality of the experience went up and places to trap became more available. It was nice to just trap during daylight hours and savor the experience a bit more. I, like many of my age, had grown up selling 'rats for fifty cents each, with kits out at a dime. To us selling them at three or four dollars still didn't seem too bad, but for many of the newly-recruited trappers who had started out with muskrats selling at six dollars, the drop in price was pretty substantial.

To be certain, many of the new trappers really enjoyed doing it, but as prices faded, they did a little less trapping. Some of those who trapped mainly for the money decided to give it up all together.

For me trapping began to occupy a place of less importance because other pursuits were paying the bills. Fortunately for me, my other business was seasonal and did allow me to get out and trap on a pretty full-time basis during the fall. I was able to acquire many of

A recent photo after a morning's run of traps in Minnesota.

Tracks in the Mud

my old trapping places again, and it was fun and a bit nostalgic to trap areas where I had grown up. I found myself really getting back into the water trapping, since that was what we had in abundance in Minnesota.

A lot of my muskrat trapping found me wading waist-deep marshes with a pack basket full of traps on my back. The feel of the soft bottom under my waders and the weight of a pack basket filled with wet muskrats strapped to my back brought back fond memories and reminded me of the extremely hard work that trappers faced.

Trapping these sloughs involved mostly setting feed beds and the large houses. Each large muskrat house was set with three or four traps placed on its outside perimeter, each staked out so they would not interfere with any of the other sets when a trapped 'rat moved the trap. These are very selective and very humane sets, with very few losses. Upon removing a muskrat from a trap, I would flip it over my back and into the pack-basket, reset the trap and move on, with my wading stick keeping me from tipping over.

As I moved along in the marsh, my pack-basket became full of wet 'rats and the water would begin to seep down my back. It was a smorgasbord for one's senses to trap a marsh. The air was filled with the smells of rich muck, algae, and sweet marsh reeds. There was the sucking sounds of boots being pulled from the slick mud, water splashing, and all of this punctuated by the staccato of migrating blackbirds and the occasional mallard. The cool feel of the water running down one's back, along with the inevitable leaking wader, gave me the feel of actually being a muskrat swimming in the marsh water. I really got a "'rat's eye" view of the marsh. The water was close to thirty-two degrees at this time of year and sometimes breaking through sheets of ice was a requirement of navigating the marsh. The sights of long, early shadows fleeing the cattails, and white frosty muskrat houses protruding from the glass-still water will always be stuck in the memory. Swimming muskrats cut wedged ripples in the pond's surface and the flaming fall colors still crowned some of the maples and oaks on the shoreline.

    Muskrat populations were very concentrated in the marshes and the catch percentages were very high the first few nights. Then the 'rat catch tapered and usually a mink or two were caught before the traps were pulled and moved to another marsh. The odds of catching the mink improved greatly as less muskrats were caught and more traps were open for the mink catch. The mink seem to move in and live in these marshes, killing and eating 'rats pretty much as they need food. The trap moving was a lot of work as all the traps and stakes need to be carried from the marsh, loaded into the truck and then carried into and reset into another location.

    During these years, our kids were growing up. As they became older, an interest developed about my trapping. They looked forward to seeing what Dad would bring home from the trap line. The skinning and stretching of the furs was intriguing to them. There were numerous occasions for learning about the biology, anatomy, and habits of the furbearers. The skinning room became a classroom. The walls were hung with beautiful furs, and again the connection between us, our ancestors, and the future could be made. Not too many kids could grow up with these types of experiences. I really believed there were life-lessons to be learned from these connections.

    The harvesting of fur became a natural and real thing for our kids. The furbearers became more than just cute furry creatures. They were shown to be part of an eternal cycle, part of a great and renewable resource. It was the species we loved and fought to preserve with habitat preservation and good conservation practices. Each catch was only a part of the species population and taking some

Tracks in the Mud

individuals a necessary part of preserving the population as a whole. I tried to show how the harvest was done humanely and selectively.

As our kids got older, they came along on the trap line as their interest moved them. They too saw the signs that pointed us to the catch—the strand of fur in a fence, the tracks in the mud, and the evidence of feeding activity. They were shown the details of the outdoors that only trappers could find. Certainly the sunsets, and the wind, and the leaves falling had a beauty that most people related to, but we learned to see the really small things that were gigantic in the world of furbearers. Hopefully we learned to see the still small world that most observers overlook.

As my son became older, he too caught the bug for trapping, and with the greatest joy I welcomed him to my trap line. To watch him as he struggled to set a number one long-spring, at first with his foot on the spring and finally by hand, was indeed touching to me. It was a great joy to pass these primal traditions to the next generation. These traditions were the most real and straight-forward ideas that we could convey. Some would contend that these are antiquated or even useless practices, yet they had served many generations and who was to say that we would ever culturally out grow our need for these traditions. Perhaps all humans would be more whole and contented if they were able to pursue the outdoor activities that trappers had the privilege to pursue.

I have always felt that it is good for children to see the real substance of the thing that their parents do. Nothing makes more sense to children than to see the setting of traps, the taking of the furbearers, and the selling of the furs that would be made into beautiful and useful articles of clothing. The tangible sense of it all hits home. There was no question about what we did or why. We didn't just go off to some mythical "office" and come home with a paycheck.

What the trapper did has the sound practicality and direction that answers children's questions by what was seen and how it was enacted. Certainly it was my hope that all of our kids would have an understanding and respect for what we did as trappers.

As my son began to spend time with me, wading steams, walking the fields, and experiencing sunrises and sunsets in places of quietude and beauty, my wish was that he too would find times of peace and contentment out on the trap line, amidst a world of constant pressure and change. On the trap line the basics never changed, the realities were a solid rock upon which we found footing from year to year and decade to decade.

There were times in the seventies when I thought the great fur boom would take the whole industry in a new direction, sweep all of us to become something we really weren't. I saw small country fur buyers become quite wealthy. There were little mom-and-pop lure makers who went "big time" in the business. New trap-making companies sprang up, and the level of participation in the whole trapping scene went over the top. The eighties and nineties showed me again that the fur industry was based in reality and founded upon reason. The exchange rate of the dollar changed, the fashions changed, and countries' economies changed. All of these factors led to declining fur markets.

The thing that has inspired me about the fur market and the trappers who supply it, is the fact that it remains. In the eighties the numbers of trappers had again been condensed to the folks who did it as naturally as getting up in the morning. Setting the steel in the late fall happened for these trappers as inevitably as the sun rose in the east. The core of trappers would harvest the fur from their areas because they knew it was a good thing, it was good for the resource, and there was a market for their beautiful product.

Tracks in the Mud

The fur boom changed nothing. The basic sets were the same, the way that furs were handled and processed hadn't changed, and the animals themselves were the same, with the same habits and populations as ever. Income for the trapper went up and came down but the basics hadn't changed. Certainly, there were less people who could earn a complete living from the fur business, but the methodology was much the same.

Perhaps the fur boom gave us all that taste of greatness that every generation of trappers deserved. A great beaver market inspired the great mountain men of old, gave the desire to explore and trap the West. Later that market crashed as beaver hats fell from favor. My dad of course talked of the great fur markets when he was young. That market also deteriorated to the low markets when I was young. So we too had our boom and it went away. Now we see spikes in certain items, or a year of good markets, followed by down times. Who knows when the next period of high demand could trigger another great market for furs.

It was a tough transition from full-time trapper to part time. No longer did I get up early and see the full expanse of the day ahead: nothing but deep creeks and rolling hills. To see the endless roll of pockets and dirt-holes, constant anticipation of Conibears filled and gold-eyed coyotes staring me down, was the pure Nirvana of the professional trapper. It was the rise of the hazy sun and the stretch of a cloudless day stalking the sunset that drove the trapper each day.

Now I choose my days to run and set and pick up the line so I can attend to other necessary duties. The endless expanse of freedom and joyful toil is broken by the necessary duties that support a family. The days of full-time profit and security on the trap line have waned.

The great joy of the part-time trap line was the act of giving the essence of the art to my son. He's had some great time to explore his own trap lines. He too spent some full days in hip boots and shoulder gauntlets, traversing the water-trap line and earning the hard money of the post-boom trapper. There was a certain toughening of the spirit that engulfed the trapper. I think it came as the northwest wind blew hard in one's face, and wet, leaking rubber gloves freeze around hands as the trapper chiseled through pond ice to check under-ice sets. Trappers were steeled by the rising mists in the early morning flashlight beam and strengthened as the late-fall skies emptied of geese and swans and only snowflakes filled the air in silent attention to the winter days.

I'm happy another trapper could see the passing of the seasons and squeeze the last goodness from the waning days of fall. A father-son bond is sealed by the freezing lakes and insulated by the first snow-blankets of the newly- insulated winter.

As we moved into the nineties, trappers became more invisible. We were much as we were before the high fur prices. The cycle had come round and again the few die-hards were out there, but many had fallen by the wayside. It seemed as though a lot of trappers just had so many other things to do. There were hunting trips to take, perhaps families to raise, or productive careers to build. To take a complete livelihood from fur production on the trap line was difficult.

A number of people began to capitalize on the abundance of animals in another way. Nuisance trapping became a profitable way to pursue the trap line full time. It was a pursuit that lent itself best to suburban and even urban areas. Wherever humans and animals mixed conflict of interest arose. Raccoons insist upon denning in buildings, skunks hole-up under porches, and bats infest attics. People who live on acreages have beaver move in and do damage to desirable trees.

The nuisance trapper must also be a master at public relations, since not all people in the urban or suburban area might agree that the animals must be removed. Of course live-trapping is an effective alternative to the conventional methods and can eliminate the offending animal without killing it. Even though the fur values have dropped, there is still a great need to keep certain animal populations in check. The savvy trapper can charge good money to remove destructive animals from an area. Trappers also do very well at pocket gopher removal. The piles of dirt caused by pocket gophers can be very costly, especially on alfalfa fields. Many counties pay good bounties on pocket gophers and landowners will add extra incentives for having those little diggers removed from their land.

Nuisance trapping may not have the glamour associated with the free-roaming fur trapper, but it can pay the bills, and I suppose there are some who run these businesses very well and make good money at it.

As we've forged into a new century, I was thrilled that we maintained our right to trap. Here in Minnesota our Department of Natural Resources and other groups have been supportive, and trappers have done a good job at education and trapper training. It's sad that the rights of trappers to ply their trade have been taken away in some states, but here we still have an active core of fine fur-takers and predator controllers.

We as hunters and trappers are criticized by the anti-trappers. We are asked the rhetorical question: "How would you like to die that way?" To them all I can do is ask another rhetorical question: "How would you like to die by starvation or disease, or by having your hamstring muscles torn out and then your guts eaten out while you were still alive?" These are the realities of life and death in nature. Nature is much more cruel than the bullet or trap of the outdoorsman.

Even if you are a vegan, you displace other creatures on this earth. Each bit of space that grows your broccoli or produces your grain displaces another creature. You, by your existence here on earth cause other creatures to die. The fact that you live here, impacts other creatures. You would have to lye down under a log, curl up, and die, to have no impact upon other animals.

We who grow food or procure our own meat only deal with the reality of survival in a personal way. We are still in touch with what it is that humans must do to stay alive in this world. It is nice that most people have others who can do the actual procurement of the essentials of life, and all they need to do is buy the commodities. How sad that many of them have the arrogance to criticize those of us who still do for ourselves. They would look down their noses at us as though we are some kind of crazy, wild throwbacks to a time forgotten. In reality, we are still connected to the heartbeat of the land and the primal song of our souls.

My son and I have run some great trap lines in recent years. Mostly we have taken a block of time in the fall, usually a week or two and run a water-trapping line. We have keyed in on 'coons, mink, and muskrats. The mixed water trap line still holds a lot of appeal for me. We've tried to hit the open water portion of the season, yet at times we end up doing some ice-trapping as well.

We've spent some awesome times in western Minnesota trapping the numerous marshes and streams. In the fall of 2006 the muskrat market actually revived quite well and we saw prices over six dollars. It happened to be a year of pretty good water levels with a decent 'rat population. We actually earned some nice Christmas money for our families. We have since done some raccoon tapping, wanting to keep the numbers in check to help the pheasant population on our farm. Raccoon have also been a great nuisance in our sweet-corn fields, and we have trapped that area a great deal.

Tracks in the Mud

Over the past twenty years there have been glimmers of hope that the fur market would rebound in a long-term fashion. In 1988 we felt fur was coming back and the world economy looked like it could support another fur boom. Then Black Friday in October dashed those hopes as stock prices fell and fur prices with them. The relatively high muskrat prices in 2006 again gave hope of a revival. As we sold our 'rats in November for six and a half dollars average there was talk about them reaching ten dollars. I know of trappers who held their muskrats and shipped to the spring auctions with high hopes of incredible prices and were disappointed when they got less than a six dollar average. The fur manufacturing industry has shifted to China and supposedly they were going to be extremely hungry for our muskrats that year. The American trapper produced muskrats in great numbers and flooded the market. That coupled with a warm winter world-wide caused less retail demand, causing muskrat prices to drop. They haven't regained the levels of November 2006 in the years since.

At this writing in 2008 we again entertain the hope of a revival. I have heard trappers say we'll have fifty dollar 'coon. Yet, the economy has really taken a down-turn, commodity prices have dropped, and recession is in the air. It is amazing how difficult it is for all the stars to align properly to produce a fur boom like we had in the seventies. I'll never be one to say it couldn't happen again, I'll not say it is a dying industry, but I do realize what a tremendous phenomenon occurred when the fur market went wild in the seventies.

The most amazing thing is that after fifty years and an unprecedented swing in fashion and resulting fur prices, I still find myself standing in the water of some lake or marsh, depressing the spring on a number one long-spring identical to the one I remember from when I was a very young kid. Some things haven't changed and I hope they don't.